Art Therapy in Practice

of related interest

Art Therapy with Offenders
Edited by Marian Liebmann
ISBN 1 85302 171 7

What Do You See?
Phenomenology of Therapeutic Art Expression
Mala Betensky
ISBN 1 85302 261 6

A Multi-Modal Approach to Creative Art Therapy
Arthur Robbins
ISBN 1 85302 262 4

Arts Therapies and Clients with Eating Disorders
Fragile Board
Edited by Ditty Dokter
ISBN 1 85302 256 X

Arts Approaches to Conflict
Edited by Marian Liebmann
ISBN 1 85302 293 4

Art Therapy and Dramatherapy
Masks of the Soul
Sue Jennings and Ase Minde
ISBN 1 85302 027 3 hb
ISBN 1 85302 181 4 pb

Art Therapy in Practice

Edited by Marian Liebmann

Jessica Kingsley Publishers
London and Bristol, Pennsylvania

First published in the United Kingdom in 1990 by
Jessica Kingsley Publishers Ltd
116 Pentonville Road
London N1 9JB, England
and
1900 Frost Road, Suite 101
Bristol, PA 19007, U S A

Second impression 1995

Copyright © 1990 the contributors and the publisher

Library of Congress Cataloging in Publication Data
A CIP catalogue record for this book is available from the Library of Congress

British Library Cataloguing in Publication Data
Art therapy in practice
1. Art therapy
I. Liebmann, Marian
615.85156

ISBN 1-85302-058-3

Printed and bound in Great Britain by
Athenaeum Press, Gateshead, Tyne and Wear

Contents

List of Illustrations

Photographs 3.1-3.5 by Dorothy Makin
Photographs 2.1-2.5, 4.1-4.5, 5.1-5.5, 7.1-7.6, 8.3-8.11, 9.1-9.2 by 'Black on White', 105 Coldharbour Road, Bristol BS6 7SD.

Acknowledgements

I would like to acknowledge the help and support of the contributors in developing this book. We would all like to pay tribute to our clients who have allowed us to use their work. My personal thanks are due also to my husband, Mike Coldham, and daughter Anna for their practical help and endless patience.

All names of patients and clients have been changed to preserve anonymity. We have obtained permission from all our clients to use their work and write about them.

Marian Liebmann

Introduction

Art Therapy and Other Caring Professions

Marian Liebmann

The idea for this book arose from the increasing number of requests for information on art therapy, as more people come in contact with art therapy and art therapists. Not only has the number of art therapists grown significantly in the last few years, but the ranges of different contexts where their skills are valued has broadened enormously. This has brought art therapists into contact with many members of other caring professions, who need and want to know more about art therapy and its benefits for their clients.

Until very recently there were no British art therapy books, and few American ones. Fortunately that situation has changed, and there is beginning to be a good range of art therapy literature. Much of this is, quite rightly, devoted to developing art therapy as a body of knowledge in its own right, and so will include a substantial theoretical component. This is useful for art therapists, both in training and working, but can be somewhat overwhelming for others who want to know about art therapy without necessarily thinking of practising it themselves. There seemed, therefore, to be a need for a book concentrating on art therapy in practice, to demonstrate its value to patients and clients, and to show some of the different ways in which it could be used.

Most art therapists have, until recently, worked mainly in psychiatric hospitals with acutely mentally ill patients. However, as hospitals close, and much of their work begins to take place in a variety of contexts in the community, so art therapists have moved to the community too. They may be found working in day hospitals, day centres, halfway houses and group homes. Although this can mean new opportunities for art therapists, there is also a good deal of insecurity arising from a fear that administrators may see art therapy as only being relevant to hospitals, and fail to recognise its benefits for patients in the community. Art therapy is still a very small profession compared with many others, and can be easily overlooked by hospital planners of patient care.

At the same time, the demonstrable benefits of art therapy for other client groups has led to an increase in its use. This is especially so for people with learning difficulties and for children, who may have inadequate verbal skills. There is growing interest in the use of art therapy for adults with learning difficulties, especially those with additional emotional problems.

Art therapy has been used for some time in special schools, but as many more children with problems remain in mainstream education, its use with children in ordinary schools is being explored. There are several examples of art therapists working with children individually or in small groups if they have behaviour problems, or are underachieving. Adolescent units and specialised child abuse teams now often use a multidisciplinary approach, and frequently include art therapists in the team. Art is a natural medium of expression for children, and art therapists are skilled in using art to help children with their difficulties.

There is increasing interest in the use of art therapy with prisoners and with offenders in community-based projects such as day centres. There is some resistance to the use of the term 'therapy' by a group which does not see itself as 'sick', but the work of helping people to acknowledge and come to terms with themselves and their problems is similar.

The current climate is one of change, whether art therapists are working under the aegis of health, education or social services. There are many stresses and strains, many of them due to the way in which systems try to arrange 'service delivery', and art therapists are not immune to these pressures. New ways of financing education, and changes in social services, may mean increased opportunities for art therapy - or the converse. In this way, all art therapists, whether working for the National Health Service or another body, have to struggle to survive.

Very few art therapists now work in individual contexts, or in an isolated art therapy department, but rather as members of a team, liaising with psychiatrists, social workers, teachers, psychologists, nurses, occupational therapists and others. Many of these colleagues have been impressed by the benefits of art therapy for their clients, and want to know more about it. Most art therapists spend considerable time giving talks and workshops to colleagues in all these professions, and this book is designed to be a contribution to disseminating information in these directions.

The Benefits of Using Art Therapy

Obviously, those of us who have collaborated to write this book are convinced of the benefits of art therapy, and anyone who has read this far is at least exploring the possibility that art therapy may be useful for certain client groups. It may still be worth listing the situations and ways in which art therapy can be particularly useful. However, it is important to remember that not all these benefits will apply to any one group, and that there may be groups or situations where art therapy is not helpful.

If therapy can be defined as 'a process of engendering favourable change which outlasts the session itself', then art therapy may be described as 'the use of art in the service of change on the part of the person who created the artwork'. It can be used with all kinds of people, and I like the phrase, borrowed from a colleague: 'No special ability or disability is needed' - just the willingness to use art materials in an exploratory way. In this respect, art therapy (especially for adults) has links with play and the use of imagination.

Some of the advantages of using art therapy can be listed as follows:

(a) Almost everyone has used art as a child, and can still do so if encouraged to forget about images having to be 'artistically or culturally correct'.

(b) It can be used as a means of pre-verbal or non-verbal communication, as a means of symbolic speech. This can be important for those who do not have a good mastery of verbal communication, for whatever reason, or for those who are 'over-verbal', as is often the case in our culture. It can help such people to look at their current situations and ways of making changes.

(c) Pictures can act as a bridge between art therapist and client, especially where the subject matter is too embarrassing to talk about, or has negative connotations for the client. In a psychotherapeutic setting, the picture may be where the transference takes place.

(d) It can be used as a means of self-expression and self-exploration. A picture is often a more precise description of feelings than words, and can be used to depict experiences which are 'hard to put into words'. It can sometimes be a good way of cutting through 'tangled verbosity'.

(e) The process of doing art can sometimes help people to become more aware of feelings previously hidden from them, or of which they were only partly aware. It can help people to become clearer when they are experiencing confusion.

(f) Using art can sometimes help people to release feelings, e.g. anger and aggression, and can provide a safe and acceptable way of dealing with unacceptable emotions.

(g) Not only feelings may be explored, but also thoughts, ideas and possible behaviour.

(h) The 'framed experience' can provide a context parallel to 'real life', to rehearse or fantasise about possible futures, without the commitment of reality. It can be used to help adults to play and 'let go'.

(i) The concreteness of the products makes it easier to develop discussion from them. It is also possible to look back over a series of sessions and note developments.

(j) Discussion of the products can lead to explorations of important issues. Pictures are often ambiguous, and the most important thing is for the creator to find his or her own meanings.

(k) Using art requires active participation, which can help to mobilise people. In a group setting, it is one way of equalising participation.

(l) Art therapy can provide an 'enabling space' in which individuals can use art materials to explore themselves without pressure. This space, together with respect for individuals and their journeys, can sometimes help people to find themselves through art therapy with only minimal intervention from the art therapist.

(m) It can be enjoyable and fun, and this may lead to individuals developing a sense of their own creativity. It can be an opportunity for adults to be allowed to 'play'.

(n) For certain disorders, it can be used diagnostically, e.g. stroke victims.

Obviously, art therapy shares some of these qualities with other therapies and styles of counselling, and can be used in conjunction with them.

The Many Forms of Art Therapy

There is continuing debate within the art therapy profession, and this is healthy. New ideas and ways of working develop, and are questioned. Established ways of working give way to new developments. New contexts for work lead to changes in attitude and practice; different client groups require different methods of working. Sometimes the debate is acrimonious, sometimes good-humoured, always interesting. I will outline some of the areas of debate where there has been the most interest in recent years.

One of the most long-running debates has its roots in the history of art therapy. This is the question of whether art therapy has more in common with art or with therapy.

Although Freud was interested in art, his work led him to see it often as evidence of pathology. Jung was much more intrigued by the creative life and his patients' pictures. He treated pictures in much the same way as dreams, as material for analysis, and as a key to the unconscious life of his patients if the images could be appropriately interpreted.

Quite separately from the development of analytical psychology, some artists took materials into sanatoria for invalids from the armed forces in the Second World War. These artists introduced painting as a form of constructive and creative occupation for people who were shell-shocked or recovering from physical injuries. They found the use of art for these patients became more than an occupation to pass the time; in fact, painting seemed to contribute actively to patients' mental healing process.

These two strands from art therapy history are still present in current practice. Some art therapists pay little attention to the process of producing a picture, feeling that the most important part of the therapy lies in the discussion of the product, and the relationship with the therapist. Other art therapists feel that the process of making an art work is the most important aspect in promoting change, and that discussing the products is largely superfluous. Most art therapists now recognise both as being important, and realise that clients may have different needs in this respect.

To illustrate this point, when I run workshops for social workers or social work students, I quite often ask (after they have done a personal piece of art work and shared it in pairs or small groups) whether they found the process of painting or discussion more important. Usually half the group find the process more important ('The painting helped me work things out, but talking about it afterwards just got in the way'), and half find the discussion the most crucial part ('I enjoyed the painting, but it was only in sharing it with someone else that I realised some of the things I had painted').

Art therapists' backgrounds also reflect this twin heritage. Most art therapists start off from an 'art' background, and feel this is important, as they know from personal experience what it is like to struggle with the art process. However, there are also a considerable number of art therapists who come to art therapy from other caring professions, such as teaching, nursing, social work or psychiatry. From whichever side they arrive, art therapists need to 'balance up' their experience while training.

Debate continues around the issue of how much 'art' there is in art therapy. Most art therapists are agreed that art therapy is not about producing 'beautiful works of art'. Rather, it is concerned with the making of art which is personal and follows internal needs and standards. Thus a scribble may be as much of an art therapy product as a completed picture. Even so, art therapists acknowledge that the formal composition of a personal statement is very important, thus emphasising the connection with art.

There is increasing interest in the use of the arts with all kinds of disadvantaged people. Many hospitals and day centres have schemes whereby artists come in and design murals, which patients and clients may help to execute. Prisoners take part in music and drama productions, people with learning difficulties are involved in movement and mime workshops. The benefits to the people involved may be far-reaching, increasing a sense of self-worth and the ability to communicate. Thus there is a continuum from arts activities to the more personal arts therapies, and it is not always easy to see where activity shades into therapy.

As a general 'rule of thumb', arts activities have as their main aim an external product (mural, concert, play, etc.), whereas arts therapies look more explicitly at the personal processes involved. This is often reflected in the initial 'contract' drawn up between the leader and the group.

From the other end of the debate, there are those from a background in analytical therapy who feel that art therapy is a derivative of more traditional analytical therapies, using paintings as well as verbal descriptions. Some of these practitioners feel that art therapists ought to train as verbal psychotherapists first and then add their art skills.

However, the art skills are not just 'added on' to traditional psychotherapy, but are part of the psychotherapy process. Art therapy may be viewed not as a derivative of psychotherapy, but more as another kind of psychotherapy or counselling in its own right. What sets it apart from other psychotherapies is both the process of drawing/painting and the use of the products. Whereas in most therapies the basis is the relationship between the client and therapist, in art therapy there is a triangular relationship between the client, the therapist and the painting process/picture. This makes work with transference more complex, and the picture adds a further dimension for projection.

This brings us to another much discussed subject in art therapy - the interpretation of pictures. Because of the historical connection with analysis, many people outside art therapy believe that art therapists' main skills are in interpreting the patients' or clients' pictures 'correctly', and assume that they have 'magical powers' to do this. However, most art therapists place more emphasis on the process of making the art products, and 'interpretation' becomes a two-way sharing between client and therapist which depends on the trust between them. Often the art therapist will concentrate on helping clients to come to their own interpretation by asking helpful questions, or by just waiting for the clients' responses to their own work.

We all bring our own particular experiences and prejudices to what we experience, and interpret new phenomena in the light of our assumptions. Art therapists, too, interpret art products in the light of their own artistic practice, their experience as therapists, and any particular theories they find helpful. Some art therapists use 'Gestalt' methods, others have a 'Jungian' outlook, others select from several schools of thought. Whatever their outlook, they concentrate on the art process, its results, and what it means for their patients and clients.

There is sometimes discussion concerning how far art therapy concentrates on conscious or unconscious material. Most artworks are products of conscious and unconscious processes, and these can be explored if it is appropriate. Often the process of making an art product brings awareness of things previously not consciously recognised, and in this way unconscious feelings can become conscious, and available for discussion.

Art therapy may be done on a one-to-one basis, or by taking part in a group. In art therapy groups all can participate at the same time in the making/painting stage, whether on individual work or a group project. Discussion of the products can take a variety of forms, and the relationship between the group members themselves can be as important as the relationship between group members and the art therapist. Working with groups requires expertise in groupwork, as well as in art therapy.

There is controversy concerning the degree of structure appropriate for art therapy groups. Some art therapists set themes to get groups started, while others feel that any external scheme or structure inhibits the personal and group therapeutic process. Here again, there is no definitive 'right' way, and different art therapists find their own positions on a continuum from structured to unstructured. Many art therapists work in both of these ways, according to the needs of the particular client group and the situation.

These are just some of the continuing debates. There is beginning to be a recognition that there are many different ways of practising art therapy, depending on the art therapist, the client group and the situation - and all may be valid and beneficial. New ways of working are being developed all the time, and art therapists are pushing out the boundaries as they do this.

Although art therapists are the most numerous, there are also drama therapists, dance/movement therapists and music therapists. In favoured situations, a therapeutic team may contain several different arts therapists, and then it is possible to combine methods from different arts. For instance, an art therapist and drama therapist may work together in a day hospital (see chapter 1), the dramatherapy session providing an opportunity to work physically on material previously raised in an art therapy session.

Although I have tried to introduce some basic concepts of art therapy here, by far the best method of explanation is to demonstrate how art therapy is used, in particular contexts and by particular practitioners, all of whom bring their own perspective to their work with clients.

The Contributors

The contributors to this volume all work or live in the same geographical region, and have met each other through regional art therapy gatherings, workshops and discussion groups. Some are close colleagues, some are friends. Some have been working in art therapy for many years, while others are relatively new. Our close geographical proximity has enabled us to consult one another over our writing, and to evolve our aims as a group.

Between us we cover a wide variety of client groups: acute and long-term psychiatric patients, psychogeriatric patients, people with learning difficulties and psychiatric problems, children with psychological problems, offenders in the community, and homeless people. Our employers include the National Health Service, an education authority, a probation service, and voluntary organisations. Our places of work range from large hospitals, day hospitals and schools to probation offices, community rooms and hostels - and the facilities vary accordingly. However, by no means do we cover the full range of contexts where art therapy is available; we have colleagues who work with alcoholics, with cancer patients, with adolescents, with physically disabled people - to name but a few.

It is impossible for any of us to present our whole practice in one short chapter, so each of us has selected one or two ways of working to write about - or one idea to follow through. Here again, there is tremendous variety, some themes being prompted by the nature of the client group or the institution, some by years of experience leading to exploration of an 'overarching' concept. Some contributors concentrate on individual work, some on groupwork, several include examples of both. Naturally, our styles of writing and presenting material will reflect our topics and our personalities.

What brings us together is a concern to find ways of explaining the practice of art therapy to the growing audience of interested people. All of us find ourselves explaining what we do to colleagues who may be psychiatrists, social workers, psychologists or nurses, for example. The following chapters try to present 'art therapy in practice' in different contexts, and thus contribute to continuing discussion in the field of art therapy. We hope it will be of interest to all caring professions and also to other art therapists.

Chapter 1

Self-Image in the Work of a Client at the Psychotherapy Day Unit

John Ford

Introduction

In adding to the many words written about art therapy, I'm aware that I may not be alone in feeling they are often indigestible. I hope that, by including a large ratio of pictures to written words, there may be more room for a balance between the 'heart-felt' and the 'head-thought'.

All models of psychology/psychotherapy attempt to reduce the 'real' into manageable quantities, and in doing so, they distort whilst also, potentially, offering tools with which to make sense of what would otherwise be a chaos of disordered information. So I am not dealing in the interpretation of symbols as absolutes, but rather in pointing out certain perspectives, for which I believe a good case can be made. Whether such perspectives are a blinding glimpse of the extremely obvious or worthwhile bits of insight clearly depends on the readers' own perspectives, but they are viewpoints that I have personally found useful in my work as an art therapist in trying to understand better both others and myself.

Working in a large psychiatric hospital, with a broad cross-section of different people with a spectrum of diagnosed problems, I came to be increasingly interested in self-images as existential statements of the 'felt-self'. 'A picture can be a more vivid and precise description of feeling than can be expressed by talking about it at length' (Fromm, 1951). In relation to the following images, the primary focus will be on the 'here-and-now' dynamics of an individual and the images produced during a short course of therapy. I selected Jean's work, both because I believe she expresses some fundamental themes to be found in the self-images of others, and also because her history illuminates the value of a holistic programme as practised at the Psychotherapy Day Unit.

The Unit Programme

People attend the Psychotherapy Day Unit five days a week for eight weeks, on a 'contractual' basis, as day patients. The unit only takes referrals from the community (as opposed to hospital residents), via community psychiatric nurses, social workers, GPs and psychiatrists working in the hospital in which the unit is based.

A policy is maintained of only working with people considered to be non-psychotic. The emphasis is on group work with little time available for individual 'one-to-one' work. Those referred are expected to attend consistently and make use of all available groups. At present, the groups on offer include a Transactional Analysis group, Psychotherapy, Drama, Art, Music, Relaxation, plus recreational time for badminton and walks. Overall, there is a strong Gestalt influence in the unit's programme.

The intention is that the groups complement one another and provide a holistic therapeutic environment. For instance, the art therapy group, an integral part of the unit's programme, is succeeded by the dramatherapy group the following morning. The art therapy group may be particularly useful in putting people more in touch with buried/repressed feelings, but is not necessarily the ideal arena to express these feelings actively and physically. It has often proved to be the case that feelings that 'surface' in art are released more tangibly and appropriately in the ensuing drama group.

The nature of the PDU programme offers a structured approach, which is intended to enable people to feel safe enough to explore difficult issues within the containment this structure can provide, and this is, more specifically, mirrored in the art therapy groups. The groups are structured in the form of an initial 'warm-up' (essentially 'how you feel' and/or 'what's on your mind') followed by a specific theme. Many of these themes encourage the expression of self-images ... e:g. how you see yourself, how others see you, how you would like to be; the animal you would most/least like to be. (Marian Liebmann's *Art Therapy for Groups* (1986) provides clarification of the use of themes in groups).

I would though, like to stress that there are no presumptions in this approach that exclude the validity of what Martina Thomson (1989) has termed the 'woolly' school of art therapy, in which clients may be offered a freer, less structured time and space, in which to experiment and experience, with minimal therapeutic intervention. Perhaps, ideally, rather than being perceived as mutually exclusive, these approaches can complement one another. As well as participating in the structured art therapy groups, those attending the PDU also have time available to paint or model in clay freely, using the facilities on offer in the Art Therapy Department.

Though there is little formal 'one-to-one' work, each client is allocated a key worker, who at the outset of PDU attendance takes a personal history. Below is a summary of Jean's history.

A Brief Family History of Jean

Jean is the youngest of four, a late 'unplanned' child, in a family of unplanned children.

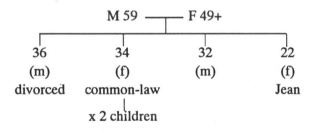

Father

Died aged 49 from kidney failure, after treatment for a long illness, (rheumatoid arthritis), contracted before Jean's birth. 'Aggression, due to illness'. Always 'tense' with Jean. 'Home life revolved around him and his needs.'

Mother

Confided in Jean. Used to talk to Jean 'as if she were an adult'. After father's death when Jean was 10, mother confided further in her and became socially isolated.

When Jean left home for college at 19 years, mother took in boarders who used Jean's old room. She was told how tidy and good they were compared to herself. After two years away, Jean returned home. Mother does everything for her at home. Jean wants to take control of her own life. A 'symbiotic relationship' is suggested by the key worker.

Siblings

Feels neglected by all three, teased by eldest of her brothers. Feels they have left her to look after mother.

Education

Three good 'A' levels. BA Graphic Design course from which Jean has taken a year out. Previously at convent school.

Psycho-sexual

'Ex-boyfriend'. Now considers herself 'too fat' to be attractive to men.

General presentation

Pale, plump, neatly dressed, always wearing black or grey, sad expression. Feels mixed up, tearful, unable to react spontaneously. Describes herself as being 'depressed' and 'withdrawn'. Says 'people should not show emotions'.

In a joint interview mother was seen to be 'infantilising' while Jean herself behaved like a little girl. (Jean later said she was unaware of this.)

The Pictures

The following pictures were produced over Jean's eight week attendance at the Day Unit. Chronologically they are in pairs, each session involving a 'warm-up' and a theme. Hence *figure 1.1a* is the first 'warm-up' and *figure 1.1b* the theme 'Regrets', both images produced in the same group session, through to *figures 1.8a* and *1.8b*, the last week's warm-up and theme. The quotes following my interpretations are Jean's own comments made a couple of years later, illuminated by hindsight and the time to digest more fully some of her experiences in therapy. (These were in response to both the pictures and my comments).

1.1a Warm-up

Presenting herself as a black sphere, lost in space. A self-image as a powerless, isolated object, almost like a head?

Jean's later comments:

I drew a series of pictures like this in my sketchbook whilst at college.

I still find the spherical shape fascinating - finding in it qualities such as - totality, independence - beauty because of its smooth surface.

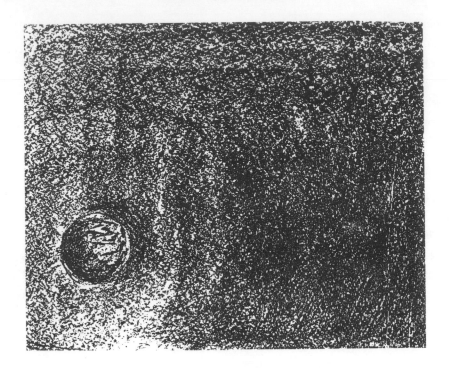

Figure 1.1a - Warm-up

Figure 1.1b - Theme: Regrets

It was extremely hard right from the beginning of the course to 'draw' anything at all, because of the analytical stance of the graphic designer, the nature of whose job it is to represent ideas in visual terms, to simplify and clarify the message to be communicated. Hence, because of my training at college I had an idea of how my drawings would be interpreted.

1.1b Theme: Regrets

She described regretting having to choose one career option, namely graphics at the expense of other possibilities, e.g. architecture.

The image reads like a row of phallic (?) railings, a barrier. How she presented at this time was very guarded, defensive and mute.

Jean comments:

> Regrets included having no role model either to imitate, idolise or rebel against. There seems to be no 'dominant lead' in my life. My mother's 'voice' was one of reason, sensibility. I resented having no one to look up to from an early age - having to find qualities of ambition (and independence?) in myself at perhaps too early an age? - not sure about this last bit, but when I think about my childhood, my strongest emotion is that I feel cheated - can't understand why people rave about school years being so wonderful, etc.

And on the use of the term 'phallic':

> I find this reference quite interesting - I am not the most feminine female I know (!) I never wear pink - I hate perfume - anything flowery - I don't believe in marriage, would never consider not having a career/job or starting a family - not at all maternal. The career I have chosen is a very male-dominated field probably because of its unsociably long hours, its uncertainty and total commitment. Am I trying to be my own dominant male lead?!

1.2a Warm-up

She presents a more tangible image of self being pulled apart by 'life stresses'. Her self-image remains faceless, anonymous, a powerless victim.

Jean's comments:

> Is it me? me/my mother? my mother? my father's illness? my powerlessness to affect any of this - to communicate with him or the world?

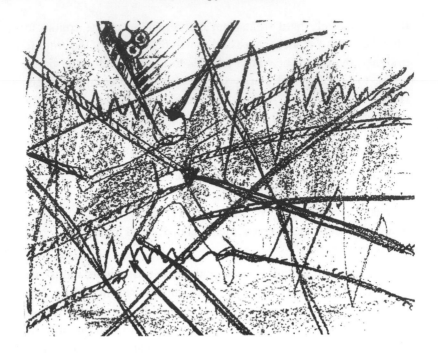

Figure 1.2a - Warm-up

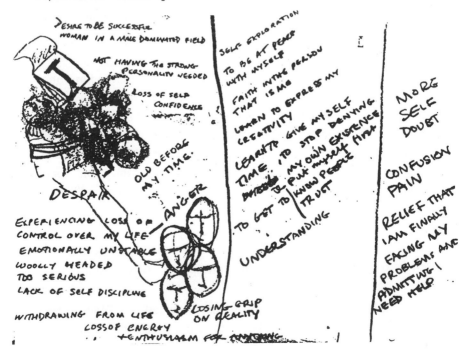

Figure 1.2b - Theme: What brought you to the PDU?

Figure 1.3a - Warm-up

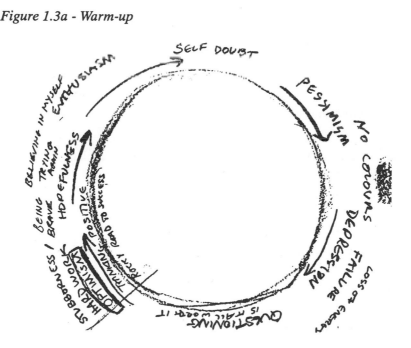

Figure 1.3b - Theme: Patterns you repeat

1.2b Theme: What brought you to the PDU? What do you want from it? What has it offered you so far?

'Male dominated field' probably implies her relationships with both her father and her brothers, (one used to tease her, and is academically very successful). Trust seems to be an important issue, implying that she has felt that her trust has been betrayed in the past.

Jean's comments:

> It seems important to me now that I think I came to understand the need for qualities such as strength, determination, ambition, (mostly shown in my extremely stubborn character) in my life at an early age. It was only later that I realised that I had not come to terms with my, perhaps, more feminine side . . . . . . I have always tended to neglect the sociable and emotional side of my character, ie other needs than those of professional recognition and self importance.

1.3a Warm-up

A self-image, again as a trapped black sphere, this time still more disempowered (and protected) by a 'cage'. Hands reaching into the picture, in her terms signified people at the PDU reaching towards her to make contact. The question mark is asking whether to let them in. There is significant colour in the others' hands compared to her black self. Taking the whole image, conceptually, as a self-image, the hands can also be seen as her own feelings surfacing, trying to make contact with the sphere as a symbol of her head. It may be also expressive of fears of physical contact in the dramatherapy group. She described problems of 'inexperience of dealing with strong emotions', and an 'inability to express my inner self.'

Jean's comments:

> Inner self neglected - not recognised as having one - I took my model
> for this from my mother - seeing her as completely self-effacing -
> do anything for anybody - etc.

1.3b Theme: Patterns you repeat

Probably a fairly universal statement of the necessity of 'ups and downs'.

1.4a Warm-up

Another black self-image, but at last a hint of 'facing' herself. A black heart, and a disembodied head. This implied separateness of her head from her heart is reinforced by 'MIND OVER MATTER', 'Headstrong', 'Intellectualising'.

Figure 1.4b - Theme

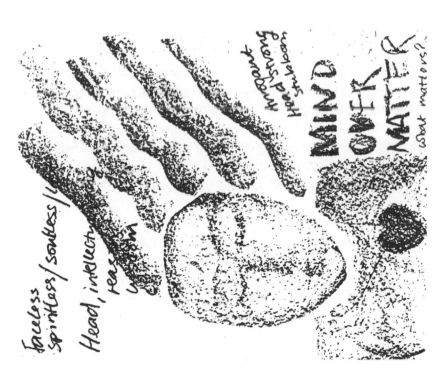

Figure 1.4a - Warm-up

Jean had had considerable feed-back in other groups about avoiding the 'felt-self' by intellectualising and excessive abstraction.

1.4b Free Theme

A classic list of depressive statements. Her anger is all turned back on to self to 'depress'. Her hands were blackened in the session with pastel - aspects of child 'messing'.

Jean's comments:

> All anger must never be shown - another aspect of my mother's character that I felt I 'ought' to adopt - years of internalising this anger, hurt, pain, led to my depressions - never 'cleaning the cupboard' as Judith (the nursing sister) terms it - by blackening my hands I was revelling in displaying my rebellion openly. I feel at this point that it is anger in a negative way - but at least to be angry at all was a step forward.

1.5a Warm-up

The boot is seen by Jean as the 'system' oppressing her. It goes with the 'not allowed', 'not eligible', 'prohibited', the 'shoulds' and 'oughts'. Self is presented as small, vulnerable, powerless. At the suggestion that this might be, also, what she does to herself, she mentioned her situation at home and her sense of feeling trapped by her mother. In an interview with her key worker, mother was described by Jean as 'on a pedestal, is perfect, cannot be criticised.' Was able to 'own her projection'; in Gestalt terms an image of 'top-dog, underdog', in Transactional Analysis terms, introjected 'critical parent' and 'adaptive child'. (For further reading on Gestalt and Transactional Analysis see references, Perls (1951, 1969) and Berne (1964) et al; see also section on 'Recurrent Themes' later in this chapter.)

1.5b Theme: A refuge and what you want refuge from

A great burst of colour in a scene from childhood on the left; it is to be hoped not just a 'going back to childhood' but an actual 'here-and-now-experience' of an aspect of herself from which she had lost contact. She looks out over a beach and the sea. The refuge is from her head, excessive intellectualising, grey matter. Perhaps the dog in her refuge symbolises the aspect of her lost animal, physical self, and perhaps to feel closer to nature is to be closer to one's own nature.

Figure 1.5a - Warm-up

Figure 1.5b - Theme: A refuge and what you want refuge from

Jean's comments:

> The holiday in the Seychelles was quite a remote, restful one, the islands were not too commercialised then - deserted beaches - leave the rat race behind, school, exams, horrid classmates, teachers etc.
>
> The dog is significant here - a wish (still unfulfilled) for a companion in life - uncomplicated, unquestioning - someone to accept me for whatever I may be - and to like me because I'm me! (Not even possible as a concept in earlier pictures).

1.6a Warm-up

A despairing image of looking down at her feet, into a threatening abyss.
Jean's comments:

> Panic, at this point in the course - I was understanding more - coming to terms with some painful truths, seeing hope, seeing more pain to make even better progress - feeling tired from all this self-examination, considering the alternatives of avoiding further helping myself, becoming aware of the fine-line nature of turning that final corner and deciding to do everything possible to get well again - to take part actively in life again - to enter adulthood.

1.6b Theme: Life Story - focus on a few major events

Very much focussed on academic, competitive achievement, and an avoidance of personal relationships themes. There is character and humour in the presentation of the chained seagull. It relates to the 'Repeating Patterns' theme. The image begs questions about what the ball and chain represent. Working on this theme further in the dramatherapy groups, they become more tangibly symbolic of her relationship with her mother, and her need to 'fly the nest'. She had left home, gone to college and partly through loneliness, returned to live with her mother where she now felt trapped. In the drama group she was able to free herself metaphorically from the ball and chain and fly; to lose her head.
Jean's comments: on loneliness:

> Mostly due to ineptitude of handling emotional situations - mistreating a girlfriend, the first significant female friend I ever had - misusing a boyfriend - ending up eventually by completely alienating both.

and

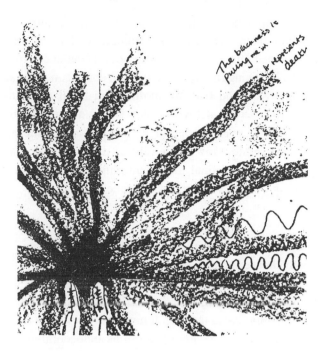

Figure 1.6a - Warm-up

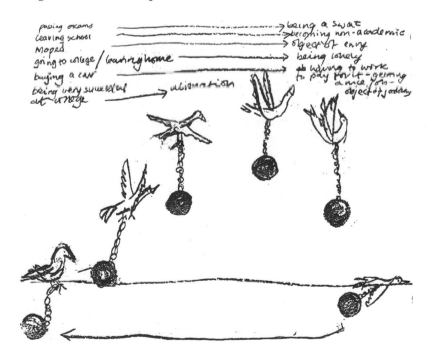

Figure 1.6b - Theme: Life story

The follow-up dramatherapy session which pursued this ball-and-chain theme was the most dramatic and significant event of my time at the PDU. It was the turning point I believe of my whole eight weeks. Realising finally that the chain connecting bird and ball was love and fear, and that my mother and I/ball and bird were interchangeable, and that love of this strength can also liberate, survive separation, even encourage it and still remain unchanged. I remember this session now as vividly as if it was yesterday - the pain and joy - and the final totally uninhibited 'flight' round the room. It is my clearest memory of my time at the PDU.

1.7a Warm-up

That there had been movement is very apparent in this image. Jean presents herself as a neatly dressed person, with *hands* and a key (both symbols of power in the world). She gives her image colour in a rainbow, to the right of her figure. It's as if her eyes are opening again. Also the 'not optimism' and 'seeing possibilities' is encouraging as the 'pendulum of emotion' has not swung 'high' out of the 'low', but implies that her perceptions are becoming more balanced. It is interesting to compare this self-image with her first as a powerless ball.

Jean's comments:

> I had not been aware of the significance of my wearing so much black and grey clothing. But it is interesting to note that now a working woman - I never wear complete black - often wearing blue jeans - red cardigan or green cardigan (not all at once!) coloured skirts, dresses - a more flamboyant expression of personality than a fashion statement. I see it as a kind of liberation - now I allow myself to dress this way - perhaps to invite attention and not to 'ERASE' myself in black.

1.7b Theme: A mask showing your real and ideal selves

Her 'ideal self' on the left is closer to a real self-image than the bloated 'real' image on the right. Also it was perhaps useful to point out that 'lonely' may be the adverse side of being 'untouchable'.

1.8a Warm-Up

A rather blank image. Listing priorities, and clarifying the confusion. At this point she was close to making a definite decision to leave home and becoming more assertive.

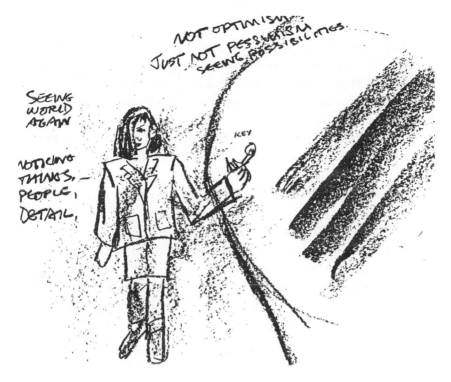

Figure 1.7a - Warm-up

Figure 1.7b - Theme: A mask showing your real and ideal selves

1.8b Theme: Gifts

Often the gifts people give to others will be projections of qualities they need themselves. This can be a useful theme both for this aspect as well as its ability to encourage people to notice and reflect on others in a group. Each group member puts their name on a piece of paper which is passed clockwise round the group for everyone in turn to draw a gift on each person's paper. When their paper returns to them, they give themselves a gift. Jean's gift to herself was the glowing red heart, a dramatic contrast to the black one she gave herself earlier. A symbol of life, love and warmth?

It is striking that, for Jean, the dramatherapy session was the most 'dramatic and significant event' of her time at the day unit, reinforcing the case for a holistic programme that can allow for the broadest range of experiment and expression. Art, drama, music and other creative, experiential approaches can complement and feed one another, and help people to liberate themselves from their many and various limitations.

The following is a quotation sent to me by Jean, with the comments she kindly offered to accompany her pictures:

> 'Only when the past ceases to trouble and anticipations of the future are not perturbing, is a being wholly united with his environment and therefore fully alive.' *(John Dewey)*

Issues for Jean

This series of images can be seen both as a part of the process of change and as a cognitive/emotive 'barometer' for measuring this. Jean's pictures tended to be abstract and cerebral (wordy). Even in the later more positive ones she still presented herself as a solitary figure. Most people spontaneously, without too many cues, tend to include important people in their lives in their pictures. In retrospect, themes such as 'Important People' , 'Mother and Father', and 'Family' could have been a useful focus for exploration. The absence of 'overt' significant others in her pictures is noteworthy, reflecting her resistance in groups to discussing specific personal relationships. However, in one-to-one work she was readily forthcoming in discussing family relationships.

Her guarded defensive style in the groups would have made it intrusive to confront her too directly on issues such as her father's death. Her wearing of black, plus the blackness of the images can perhaps be seen as working through unresolved grief. Jean states 'Perhaps the grief was for the childhood I never had. The holiday snaps of my parents, brothers and sister before I was born. I

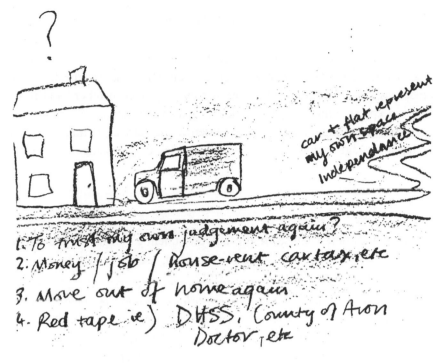

Figure 1.8a - Warm-up

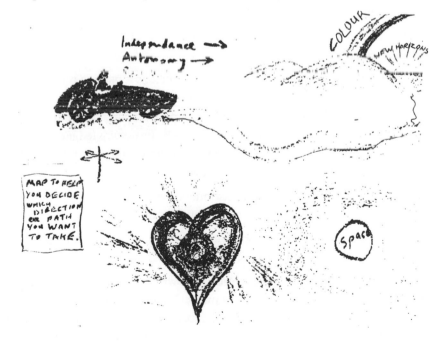

Figure 1.8b - Theme: Gifts

was too young to remember holidays with the family before my father became ill'.

She was able during her time at the PDU to confront not just her own dependence on her mother, but her mother's on her. Jean became far more relaxed, less concerned about the need for the approval of others and more willing to express opinions that would risk alienating others. She came to a decision about working towards independence and leaving home, and after returning to college, gained a good degree, and is now pursuing a successful career.

Recurrent Themes

As explained earlier, I chose to present this client's images in particular, because they express visually some fundamental, archetypal themes, as described below.

Loneliness *(see 1 (a) in particular, though 'alone' in other images).* 'What is madness? A kind of loneliness.' (Rory Macleod, 1988). Whatever diagnostic labels people are given, a sense of aloneness in their suffering seems virtually fundamental. Whether isolation comes from 'illness', or 'illness' from isolation, the need for contact and communication is implicit.

Barriers *(see figures 1.1b and 1.3a).* Learned protective defences may also imprison and isolate.

Self as Victim *(see figure 1.2a).* If self is presented as a passive puppet, then who pulls the strings? The client's perception is that this is what the world/others do to her, that she is being pulled apart, whilst also being a statement of what she is doing to herself, unacknowledged. To have had violence (emotional or physical) imposed on one may lead to introjecting the pattern of doing likewise to oneself.

The Prisoner *(1.3a).* Symbols of imprisonment beg questions as to who built the walls of the prison and what constitutes these barriers.

Disembodiment *(1.4a).* Being trapped in one's head, split off from a physical sense of self, can be a form of avoiding the 'felt-self'.

The Bad Child *(1.4b and 1.5a).* As Dorothy Rowe (1983) argues, suppressing anger is a recipe for de-pressing oneself (pushing oneself down). One reason for suppressing anger is to perceive it as bad and then oneself as bad for feeling anger. This suggests that parental/cultural imperatives to this effect have been introjected during childhood, and taken on board for the future.

'Critical Parent/Adaptive Child'. 'Top Dog/Underdog' *(1.5a)*. These essentially parallel concepts taken from Transactional Analysis (Berne, 1964) and Gestalt Therapy (Perls, 1969), respectively, bear a strong relationship to the Freudian 'Super-ego' and 'repressed Id.' These metaphors are models for describing the living psychic dynamics of an individual, in which there may be conflict between the part of self which says, 'you should, ought, must not, etc.' and the repressed primary needs of a human being, including that of self-expression. The symbol of the 'boot' in this image represents a projection on to others of the Critical Parent/Top Dog aspects of self. It can prove helpful to a client to encourage them to experiment with 'being', that which in the image is defined as 'other', enabling them to 'own' split-off parts of themselves.

The Black Hole *(1.6a)*. This symbol may represent death, disintegration and the 'unknown', but the death may also be of parts of the old self to enable the new to be born.

Flight *(1.6b)*. The theme of flight/escape complements that of imprisonment, and poses questions as to what is being fled? There are risks of flying too high, getting one's wings burnt, not having one's feet firmly on the ground, but, more positively, freedom from past patterns.

Facing of Self *(1.7a)*. A face with eyes open, hands, a complete body; here is a much more integral self-image, implying a cooler, more objective, adult, and balanced looking at self.

Clearly these themes are interrelated, derived as they are from breaking down a mass of information about a whole process and person into manageable bits. This involves a necessary reductionism. If some of the themes described are the 'blinding glimpses of the obvious' of which I forewarned, then this familiarity may be an indication of their pervasiveness, both psychologically and culturally. For example, the theme of 'Critical Parent/Adaptive Child' contains the elements of Oppressor/Oppressed with consequent political implications. So, whilst not wishing to devalue the political implications of this motif, it is important to be aware of a client's self-oppression, which is frequently denied through their being trapped in playing the 'Blame Game', ie 'Someone else is *totally* responsible for my feelings.'

Concluding Comments

There is a significance in the choice of 'Jean' as a pseudonym for the client which struck me on having completed this chapter; 'Jean' is French for John. I can identify personally with the themes, and the struggles expressed through them, which reinforces a sense of the power of symbols; that they can bring together the personal and the universal.

I hope Jean's example demonstrates the value of a holistic approach, in which art therapy practised in isolation may not be sufficient in itself, needing other approaches both verbal and physical to complement it. I believe, on the basis of experience, that most individuals will select, themselves, what is useful and helpful to them from a range of approaches and interventions.

It is notoriously difficult to prove the effectiveness of the various psychotherapies, and worth noting the range that word encompasses from the psychoanalytic couch to the 'primal scream' of encounter groups. Perhaps the best evidence of the effectiveness of an approach is to listen to the voices of those that have experienced it, and this can include listening to the images themselves, the 'voices of silence'.

Chapter 2

Valuing the Middle Ground
Art Therapy and Manic Depression

Roy Thornton

Introduction

In this chapter I try to open a window on the way painting approaches relate to the psychiatric problems presented to the therapist. I concentrate on the methods I use, without entering into the details of cases or imagery. I have chosen one client group - those suffering from manic depression - to illustrate one approach. While some features of their distress are particular to this client group, they are not all exclusive to them; my responses, equally, are not exclusive, and I suggest that some of the ideas can be used with other people.

I work in a psychiatric hospital, two day hospitals, and an out-patients clinic in a general city hospital. The referrals come from GPs, psychiatrists and other professionals, and people can refer themselves via a GP. People can come as individuals, as a family, as couples, or join a therapy group, and often use a combination of these. The door remains open at the end of therapy, and people can ring up if necessary to continue the process and help prevent unnecessary deterioration and readmission.

I am faced with people in pain and distress; I work with and through the distress, using a process of painting and talking with the person to restore a sense of meaning and value to their life. People are often surprised to find that, during the process of therapy, suffering and disaster become 're-framed' as an opportunity to learn, and they see their living experience within a different framework.

It is interesting to note that the Chinese ideogram for suffering and disaster is made up of two characters - one for tragedy, the other for opportunity. So in response to 'negative' events, the victim/beneficiary is encouraged to respond creatively, and to see that suffering may be a harmful misdirection of energies which can be restored as a beneficial source. For example, the colour red in an early painting may be described by a client as anger; the same colour in a later painting may be used to convey vitality itself.

When I first started working in psychiatry it was thought that psychotherapy had nothing to offer to sufferers from manic depression, and that management by drugs was the only answer - a view I have always challenged. Now I find that people are requesting a much deeper understanding of their state and experience; they also want support in regaining a position of responsibility for their lives. These have always been important themes underlying the direction of my work.

Manic Depression

People who are diagnosed as manic depressive experience drastic changes of mood from 'highs' to 'lows' of varying intensity. Highs are sometimes eu-

Figure 2.1 - Life story of manic depressive sufferer

phoric states in which people are highly active. They talk a lot, think rapidly, act restlessly and are unable to focus. There is a feeling of higher energy and endurance, and an expanded sense of self. People may become dominating and threatening (even assaulting others), or they may hallucinate and become deluded. Moods may change suddenly.

This is shown by *figure 2.1*, a manic depressive sufferer's expression of their life story. The colours used are mainly black and yellow, with flashes of red in the central band. Most sufferers tell me the black refers to lows, the yellow to good times or highs, and the red to frustration. We can see from this picture the dramatic changes of amplitude in the experience of sufferers.

The euphoria in a high may include experiences similar to those described in accounts of spiritual experience: being in the presence of God, or being absorbed into him.

I have known people in manic phases to order twelve Rolls Royces, buy a thousand dolls, become suddenly sexually promiscuous, or try to fly from a cliff. They bitterly regret their actions in the subsequent crushing lows. Highs clearly have their drawbacks!

Lows can be immobilising: the person feels worthless, unmotivated and robbed of all energy. In this state people are withdrawn and can be a danger to themselves. Both states are potentially dangerous, and anger features in both.

I do not see people for therapy who are too inaccessibly high or low: if they are too low they are unable to engage, and when high they are too distracted. I can begin to work when they are coming into the middle ground.

I usually start to work with someone who is anxious not to re-experience an extreme mood swing, having come down from a high; is fearful of the almost inevitable subsequent low; or who cannot bear a repetition of dropping into a low in a pattern of lows. This anxiety can fuel the determination to go through the difficulties of therapy.

In my response to manic depression I draw attention to that central area of experience which manic depressive sufferers have such difficulty valuing: the area between emotional extremes - the middle ground.

The Middle Ground

The 'middle ground' is a term I use to describe the area of experience between a high and a low. In this area one can respond to life without being unduly influenced by internal mental factors or external 'reality' events. Manic depressive people often lack insight and flee from internal mental events into 'reality'. The middle ground is an area in which self-acceptance and self-awareness leave a person less vulnerable to anxieties and more able to check these against reality.

Some Theories of Manic Depression

It is perhaps worthwhile at this stage to attempt an explanation of why these difficulties may arise. Not everyone responds to pressure and unhappiness by means of manic depressive reactions, so the question arises as to how this happens to some but not others. Something I have found to be of great value is to look for the initial trigger to the most recent high or low state: often people who are manic depressive cannot see the causal connections for themselves and need assistance to do so.

We are all highly affected by our parents; those born into a manic depressive family, with its sometimes dramatic and unpredictable behaviour, can be hugely influenced by such experience.

Another thread I see is the effect of parental love being conditional on attainment. In this situation, unless people achieve whatever their family values, they risk being deprived of life-giving nourishment such as acceptance, warmth, love and recognition. This immediately raises a number of unhappy problems. If attainment within the family model gets a positive response, it is sensible to conclude that it is the external 'successful' activity that is acclaimed, but not the individual as such. It follows that it is not enough to be yourself, you are under pressure to be 'more adequate' in some way. Since success needs perpetual demonstration, life becomes a kind of 'running-of-the-gauntlet' in which failures are punished by re-experiencing being of little value - not worth even conditional love.

This gives rise to anxiety about performance, and focuses on it. No action is neutral or safe, but is a point-winner for conditional love. Fear of failure threatens performance, affects any pleasure involved, and can sap volition. People can become completely taken up with themselves, their appearance, their self-worth. The sufferers need continual reassurance as to their value, and may feel compelled to look for successful people on whom to model themselves and gain acceptance. They often have one greatly-admired person from whom they need gratification and emotional security. However, they may also envy and resent their model, although they cannot admit this, as the model is the source of good things. This repressed aggression can lead to a loss of energy which threatens the ability to succeed. Thus self-defeat arises as a tactic to avoid envy, while success is still required to gain approval.

Our needs should be met by physical and emotional support in infancy, and when they are not, people may resent those who have what seems to be denied to them. This can lead to a need to compensate, whether in the world of fantasy or the real world of parents or their substitutes. For instance: we may struggle for gratification in reality, make fantasy come true through power, money, sexual success, or by attracting attention; we may overrate ourselves, knowingly or not, and withdraw in a stance of superiority; or we may develop some form of gaining approval.

As part of this compensatory activity, people may avoid and deny their internal experience of insecurity and put increased value on their external world. This leaves them so vulnerable to external influences that a setback from this source can completely scuttle them and precipitate a manic or depressive episode.

The source of the setback may appear quite inconspicuous to observers, yet be sufficient to create the crisis. The sufferer has been attending only to the outside world, and so is unlikely even to notice any inner reactions to those outer 'negative' events, let alone see the connection and its significance. This is a very dangerous state of ignorance for the person, and if practitioners also miss those links they may not make sense of the precipitating factors.

To sum up, then, a setback in the outside world can lead to a low, or the evasion of that low by a flight into a high. The person experiences the low as a failure and loss of worth, which then provokes further negative judgement and helps to feed a negative spiral. The high courts serious dangers through uninhibited acts, with the alienation that follows from exaggerated behaviour.

I hope this description shows how, for sufferers of manic depression, the space between extremes has never existed and so is of little apparent value. For someone who feels attractive only as an achiever, this 'middle ground' experienced by others who have been loved for themselves is 'too ordinary'. It is not an adequate place to be, and staying there seems to them to be failure and thus itself a source of anxiety.

The challenge for any therapist, therefore, is to enable the sufferer to establish this 'middle ground' of experience as being of value, in which the person himself or herself is sufficient, without having to 'perform' to merit positive regard from others.

The sufferer may well have to rediscover and revalue his or her internal world, including those feelings of insecurity which he or she had learned to fear. This can be difficult for a person who has become oriented outwardly, who denies the inner world, sees intimacy as fraught with dangers, and thinks in black-and-white terms.

The painting tasks I suggest to sufferers are designed to draw their attention to the 'middle ground' and its attendant issues. Clearly people must be in a state where they can make use of, and learn from, these approaches. Here medication may have a role until other means are developed to bring a person within reach of psychotherapy.

Initial Interview

In the initial exploratory interview I pay particular attention to *the circumstances immediately before each crisis*, especially the most recent episode.

This material must then be explored to draw out the client's particular reactions, his reading of the experience, and the roles of significant others. This cues the therapist into the client's thinking, and also focuses on a live issue of current concern to the client, and which can contain many points to learn from.

Art Psychotherapy Techniques and Processes

Although the random use of themes in an inexperienced and uncoordinated way has little to offer, I find that sometimes judicious interventions can yield much earlier movement of a creative nature than 'non-directiveness'. At other times I emphasise the value of leaving people to discover their own direction by being left free to paint, especially since we wish to encourage people to rely on their own capacities.

The following accounts of themes and procedures indicate a resource of choices with which the therapist may respond to manic depression. Some may be used repeatedly, perhaps with adjustments or variations, but in no slavish order, and should always be offered as suggestions without obligations. They are not intended as a recipe for directions. They have been distilled from contact with patients over many years.

Unless the initial interview throws up something more compelling, I start by suggesting that the person paints without guidance from me. This usually clarifies several issues, locates some of the therapy areas, and influences my hypotheses.

For example, these sufferers are often overly concerned about order. This is likely to show up in a number of ways, such as a tendency to prefer pencils or crayons to paints, to use straight lines or stripes, dots, symmetrical compositions, geometrical patterns, outlines, flat colours, with little or no colour mixing or texture. Obsessive people often hesitate to start; they plan, proceed carefully, and worry about their performance - whilst emotion, if expressed at all, usually appears in a restricted form.

Art 'standards' and 'rules' worry many beginners, and I go to some lengths to reassure them, saying perhaps that this is not 'Art', that I am not interested in their performance, and that talent is not important. This usually relaxes painters and they are likely to paint much more freely. If trust between us develops, they will often paint with surprising honesty, immediacy - even courage and power - and these qualities become valued more than pleasing effects. This of course is relevant to the manic depression sufferer, who fears that failure might mean loss of love; or that success would create envy, and this would court the same result.

The positive responses of the therapist and group members to a person's attempts towards authentic expression give a manic depressive person the confidence to alter his or her value system from an outward orientation towards inner concerns and their realities.

After a good look at the features of a first picture, the painting approach I most frequently suggest next is one which uses wet paper and let-down paint: the paper is soaked through with water, and water-based 'Redimix' is let down (mixed with water). I then encourage the painter to play with paint on the paper, without concern for content or end result, but with attention perhaps simply on how the pigment runs, blends and creates its own unexpected patterns and effects. This apparent 'non-art' approach usually draws the painter unselfconsciously into a deeper level of absorption than one where deliberation is predominant.

A further suggestion may be offered, that if the painter sees patterns or recognisable forms in the visual effects produced, or if he or she observes feelings arising in the process, these may be developed if wished.

Alternative methods may include making 'as much of a mess as possible on the paper', which can involve manipulating the paper itself, perhaps 'destructively' or to 'work as fast as possible', perhaps to cover all the whiteness of the paper. These are extremely useful loosening-up and engaging processes which have many advantages for most client groups, except those who are too rigid and react too defensively. If entered into willingly, these techniques can open up several creative avenues: a sense of fun, delight, focused attention, excitement with invention of variety, spontaneity, panache, feelings, and an approach to form that arises from a deeper level than deliberative thinking.

This is likely to offer the manic depressive client a novel experience, in which he may live vividly through attentive action, in the present, on the paper before him. Feelings can be more readily expressed, fairly easy to identify and so available to discuss in group or with the therapist. A few clients, however willing they may be, are unable to connect with the process in the early sessions. In response, I have found that 'fast painting' is useful since it excludes time to think and emphasises attention in the present. A recent client described his experience with pleasurable surprise as rather like 'being catapulted into the Now'.

It may be seen that these techniques which emphasise process rather than theme (that is, the complex interactions between painter and surface via paint), can have multiple effects both of visual interest and therapeutic benefit. Through these often intense interactions, which can have the quality of 'dreaming whilst wide awake', much inner activity is manifested and made available for discussion. The object is not to 'produce material for discussion' - a popular misconception - but rather the vital activity of the painting process itself. There is also, of course, within each separate painting, and also in the continuum of paintings, much of additional value to discuss. We also have an extraordinary record, more available than dreams, to help us share and explore, sometimes painfully, this variously hidden material.

These methods allow people to experience the 'middle ground' with increased awareness of feelings and inner values, and also the ability to express it vividly and spontaneously. In a group situation the painter has the benefit of seeing others paint, and from this can reflect on his own responses. A recent manic depressive client noticed that he could not 'get into' his painting; he stereotyped his approach with a formula of stripes, varied only with colour. He was similarly unable to 'get into' his life. The loosening approaches produced a 'just-a-mess' response, whilst paradoxically he often appreciated the vivacity of others' freer paintings.

Family Conflict and Related Themes

Whilst people often protect themselves from painful past experiences, and their inability to resolve these, by saying 'You can't alter the past', they often still carry their past with them in ways that detrimentally affect current experience. Strategies which were understandable, even necessary, in early life may have damaging effects in current situations, e.g. it may have seemed advisable to keep quiet to avoid unpleasant or violent responses in childhood, but in a marriage this unresponsiveness can lead to frustration in a partner, and ironically may reproduce the very pains the spouse wishes to avoid.

With this in mind, family-related themes can be invaluable. I mention briefly two themes, and then explore the third more fully.

Cartoon strips, montage scenes, paintings or drawings, may be used to illustrate a life story. Whereas the wet paper technique reveals much that is relatively inchoate, this task is more focused and may begin to show the dynamics of the family-of-origin - dynamics which may well illuminate the current difficulties. Significant events are likely to be present, though some may be repressed or 'forgotten'. I would expect to see clues about the quality of the painter's life experiences. In a group there is also a good opportunity for the person to see how he was 'trained' or conditioned, how his life-script compares with other group members, is particular to his family, and how it might be re-evaluated.

It might be useful to look more closely at one of the family 'set pieces', such as the 'family-on-holiday', or simply the 'family-at-home'. These give much additional information as to how the family is structured, its degree of closeness, warmth and involvement, together with alliances, coalitions and exclusions, as well as the general quality of family life.

The theme I would like to describe in detail focuses more directly on issues of conflict (and its avoidance) within the family. This is an important theme in family life, and care has to be taken in considering the person's and group's readiness to handle such strong emotional material. If the therapist is confident that both therapist and client or group can cope with their responses, this theme often proves to be a turning point in therapy.

Patterns of conflict-resolution in families are crucial to the success of the family in developing and maintaining a climate in which all its members may express themselves freely, and respond to each other creatively.

I would say that most of my clients are in therapy because of unhappy family politics in their family of origin. These dynamics continue to affect the client, and may be imported into the next generation, to continue the cycle of pain and frustration.

The theme I ask clients to consider is 'a moment of conflict in the family'. When introducing this, I point out that conflicts in life are inevitable, and illustrate this from the wide range of potential differences, such as experience, values, histories, feelings and thoughts, let alone the wishes of two people at any one moment. The chances of agreement on all possible points of difference are remote - hence the need for such valued human qualities as love, patience and sympathy. To dare to notice differences from one's parents or spouse can require considerable courage because it may raise all sorts of experiential 'ghosts'. For example, to disagree might be read as being a nuisance, naughty or nasty, right through to being in need of treatment; the penalties being drawn from all forms of pain, including rejection, that is withdrawal of the 'good objects'.

It is common in therapy to discover anger towards a parent; manic depressive men often discover anger towards their father. I may suggest that they address this directly in paint, and then talk to their father in the painting concerning their anger. This may be as near as they can get to talking to this parent, or may facilitate direct discussion in a family meeting later.

That defences developed in childhood are not always relevant in adulthood often seems a novel concept to clients, especially as they are often unaware of these defences. People find themselves caught in the dilemma of whether to continue with their habitual 'protection rackets' that offer only short-term security, or face the alternative road to more vivid living, filled initially with spectres of redundant guilt, punishment, rejection, or worthlessness. At such moments, hope may become centred on the therapist, who must not soften the dilemma to the extent that the person is robbed of their own struggle to face pain and fear. However, if trust has been established, or in a group discussion enough common ground is shared, people will make their moves.

It is at this time that one sees the value of suffering construed as both tragedy and opportunity, when some of the best human qualities appear in the face of fears of many kinds.

However, it is not enough to confront others with conflict situations: I must also act sensitively to increase the chances of a successful outcome, and at least maintain the relationship. Often clients confuse the person criticised or criticising with the item of behaviour in question, and this undermines communication. Another common problem is that of ensuring that 'message sent' is 'message received'. These misunderstandings form the material of many exchanges in individual work, guidance for couples, group work and family therapy.

The painter is encouraged to look into this fearful, yet rewarding, area of inner life - past, yet still very alive - by remembering a moment of conflict in the family of origin. I often meet people who play 'happy families' and deny any such experiences. Perfect families still have to deal with differences, so how do they avoid conflict? Perhaps one calls the tune and the other passively agrees. Maybe they retreat into 'hard work routines', or project their hostilities outwards on to 'bad objects'. Sometimes they find a family 'scapegoat' whose eventual craziness 'makes sense' of the distorted ways of relating. To help a painter make contact with the realities of his family's politics, I sometimes suggest he recalls a family atmosphere, or simply the ways in which his family makes decisions.

It is hardly surprising that many paintings look like battle grounds. However, many are cold or bleak; for example, the family may be drawn as fragmented: in order to avoid further pain, adults and children withdraw to their separate womblike rooms.

The painting experience itself may be painful, but in sharing this in a group, and exploring the dynamics of the family, the painter can begin making sense of hitherto perplexing and hurtful experiences. He is then able to clarify his own responses, notice the unhelpful strategies he may have developed, and differentiate between the short-term value they had at that time, and the harmful long-term effects outside the family.

A recent client explored in several paintings the model of his original family, which hinged around 'strengths and weaknesses'. He saw how he had imported something of this into his current family, and how this conflicted with what he wanted. By painting in a 'safe' diagrammatic way, he clarified the family's influences, and so helped liberate himself from their spell.

Optimism in therapy arises when I can see the route clearly from these early family difficulties to their resolution in the present. It would be cruel simply to highlight a person's shortcomings and those of their family. Compassion is involved in understanding how people can become caught unwittingly in knotted family webs, but this is hollow unless effective guidance is available to untangle the web.

The family conflict theme can be followed with one that highlights how current conflicts are handled, simply by asking the person to recall a recent example. If the feelings have cooled with time, I ask the person to relive it and then paint this experience.

Group Paintings

Another approach involves the whole group simultaneously in a more immediate 'here-and-now' experience. The group is presented with materials and a large area of paper (say 2m square), without any further direction. The immediate effect of this approach is that the painters are deprived of the comfort of their own 'islands of paper'. There is no clearly defined boundary, no definition of personal space. This seems promptly to raise the related anxieties of intimacy, distance and hostility. It is a primitive and basic conflict situation where attack, defence, withdrawal, denial, fear and anger all play a part. These feelings may be denied at the outset, as people paint in the immediate space in front of them, delaying painting near their neighbours, or in the centre of the whole sheet. Each person's area reflects something of themselves, but as neighbouring areas of paint spread, so concern intensifies around the remaining spaces. Some avoid all contact by restricting their painted surface; some put clear barrier lines to limit the approach of others and mark out their personal space; others may overlap tentatively, boldly, or even aggressively. Each move is a comment on how personal spaces might be understood and valued, and how far their neighbours' actions are acceptable.

The completed picture may reflect the group's development in a number of ways. At best, it may be a picture of such unity, vigour and luminosity that little more could be desired; often, however, it expresses an earlier stage of a group's development. So there may be nervous spaces, defensive lines, or intrusive gestures, which give their own messages, and may disrupt the visual unity of the picture.

Occasionally a group wishes to appear unified by producing a superficial overall effect. However, this can usually be discerned as they show their lack of genuine involvement by using impersonal dots, coolness of colour, diagrammatic lines and shapes. Sub-groups may reveal themselves in the way people's painted areas merge easily; and sometimes people imitate others' images.

An unevenness in the final overall image may reflect imbalances in the group, such as different stages and developments of individuals, as well as different levels of willingness, or ability to create intimacy.

Not everything in the minds of the group members is explicitly painted. In a recent group, one member painted in black a plan of a 'maximum-security prison cell'. This was entered by a line painted tentatively by another group member. Nothing further appeared in paint; but the following discussion revealed that the first painter was extremely angry at what she saw as an insensitive intrusion into her area - an illustration, perhaps, of how much an area of paint can mean to its author.

I use a group painting session to engage clients more closely with the issues of conflict and intimacy. It is usually wise to follow this up with at least another session to allow for further work on these issues.

Assessment of Progress

Manic depressive sufferers often show a lack of social insight into their effect on others. Some feel they express themselves inauthentically, and this shows up in their early painting in therapy, in their use of stereotyped lines and shapes. Their neighbours in a group painting may find it difficult to respond to these visual expressions.

Figure 2.2 - Cautious attempt at expression of feelings

Figure 2.3 - Explosive release of emotion

Manic depressive sufferers, whilst being superficially social, may strike discordant notes of separateness in group-related behaviour. Progress with a manic depressive client can often be assessed visually from the degree of 'deliberative painting', for example, striped rainbow quadrants in rather arbitrary colours. These contrast with paintings which immediately strike me as 'engaged', where lines have energy and vitality, colours are more personal, suggestive of a clear mood or feeling. (This must not be taken to mean that all carefully-constructed works of art are symptoms of manic depression!) An increase in spontaneity and personal expression in a manic depressive sufferer's painting is often followed by the same qualities appearing in the painter's personality.

The pictures I have chosen demonstrate the different stages in this process, from a cautious start through an explosive release to a calmer acceptance.

Figure 2.2 shows the painting of a group member, and is an attempt to portray freely their current feelings. However, it is a carefully constructed picture which refers to feelings rather than actively expressing them.

Figure 2.3, by contrast, portrays much more directly the artist's current feelings of explosive frustration, and wish to 'break out', together with a fear of the possible destructive consequences. It is painted in black, yellow and red. It represents a crucial turning point in therapy - a more authentic engagement - but there is much further work still to do.

Figure 2.4 is an example of a painting towards the end of a period of treatment. The person has got in touch with their emotional life and become much more at home with their feelings. This results in a greater range of colours, depth and subtlety - in this case purples, blues, greens and golds, with gradations in between.

Figure 2.5 is a more lively painting from the later part of therapy. It shows the artist's new-found freedom, but maintains a sense of cohesion. The strong creative element in the picture has been paralleled by personal development in terms of greater warmth, sensitivity and appropriate assertiveness.

The more 'engaged' paintings may reflect a shift of attention from reliance on other people's standards to the painter's discovery of their own resources. When this happens, it is clear that something very significant has occurred, and I support the changes by continuing to work within the relatively safe environment of painting.

One of the ways in which I encourage individuals at this stage is to explore their anxieties about asserting themselves in situations of possible conflict. The aim is to help them to relate more honestly to other people - whether parents, spouse, colleagues or friends. Often further work is needed concerning clients'

Figure 2.4 - More mature expression of feelings

Figure 2.5 - Freedom with cohesion

fantasies of being destroyed, destroying, or remaining unheard. Skills of diplomacy and assertiveness may need to be taught or discussed. However, as this lies outside the brief of this chapter I will not elaborate further, except to stress its importance in preventing re-admission to psychiatric hospital.

Manic depressive sufferers may need follow-up for some time, since they show a continuing tendency to serious mood changes, without being readily able to spot the immediate cause. However, enabling the person to practise tracing mood-origins, and responding appropriately to them, usually results in diminishing needs for further assistance.

Conclusion

I have chosen to illustrate my work as an art therapist by looking at the ways in which I work with a specific group of clients - manic depressive sufferers.

These clients are often stuck in responding to stressful situations by falling into a 'low', or avoiding this by a flight into a 'high', and have lost touch with the 'middle ground' in between. Frequently their loss of insight and mistrust of emotion leaves them very vulnerable to external influence. This is often linked with manic depressive families of origin, and with families where love is conditional on external achievement. I have described how art therapy can be used to help manic depressive sufferers to begin to value and trust their internal world through painting, and thus become less vulnerable.

It is delightful to see people who are initially too trapped in desperately tragic life scripts, liberate themselves and attain a fresh authenticity and sense of meaning in their lives. They understand themselves and others more fully, and interpret social interactions more beneficially.

They have explored experiences from their families of origin, transference issues, communication problems, matters of self-image, conflict resolution and the arts of self-assertion. They will also take away with them skills for further self-development and an increased ability to respond effectively in their lives.

The quality of painting by manic-depressive sufferers can also be a barometer, recording their progress, which may then manifest itself in their behaviour. Art psychotherapy has a particular contribution to make in encouraging the spontaneity and freedom of expression which are needed to help bring about the changes I have mentioned. The process of painting is just as important as the discussion that follows.

All of this elevates sufferers from the position of victims of tragic destructive circumstance and experience, to that of people who can respond to the challenges of life and have richer inner and outer lives. They will have learned a great deal.

Chapter 3

The Revolving Door
The Day Hospital and Beyond

Claire Skailes

Introduction

Working in a county psychiatric hospital at the beginning of the 1990s, one is aware that it is a time of change - dramatic change, as in a few years the large Victorian building will close and be replaced by smaller, more accessible units. The present day hospitals will be developed into resource centres where a wide range of therapies will be available. This will bring the treatment of mental illness out of its isolation into the community, and will, one hopes, reduce some of the fears and stigma surrounding it.

In recent years there has been quite a change in the approach to patients while in hospital. Now, it is not just a case of treating symptoms and containing the illness; there is an upsurge of interest and experience in various therapies and in counselling. Patients are encouraged to work with their problems, to find means of coping with anxiety and stress and to explore ways to change their attitudes towards life. Art therapy has developed considerably and there are now four art therapists where, only a few years ago, I was the only one. My own work has its base in analytical psychotherapy which is now well accepted; not so long ago it was hardly taken seriously. Despite the developments in treatment there are still patients who leave hospital, but after some time need to return there. It can become a recurring event, and with each subsequent admission patients become more dependent. This circular journey from hospital to day hospital, out into the community and back to hospital leads to the title of this chapter 'The Revolving Door'. In this chapter I shall describe the work of two art therapy groups; one that takes place in the day hospital; the other, which has developed out of the day hospital group, takes place out in the community. By viewing these I hope to show how art therapy may be used to aid full and permanent recovery.

The Day Hospital

The day hospital is a friendly place where patients come for various sessions - for example, anxiety management, relaxation and coping with stress. Amongst these sessions is an art therapy group which lasts for one hour and takes place in a room which is far from suitable for therapy; it is much too small and is surrounded by outside distractions. Just because art therapy has been given so little space, I feel it is important that this space is used effectively and that the group is integrated with the work of the day hospital. I rely on the day hospital staff to refer patients to the group and often these are people who find it difficult to join in the other groups and activities. A majority have difficulties in communication and expressing themselves verbally. Some, however, have a good facility with words and use them with some skill, intellectually and in defence, to block off their feelings. There are patients who sit stolidly frozen, quite certain that there is nothing that can be done for them, convinced that there is no point in trying to do anything for themselves. Most patients suffer from some form of depression.

Bringing this collection of people together to form a group is quite a daunting prospect. I enter the room, which is very small, and am confronted by a cloud of leaden heaviness. I am aware of the patients' apprehension, anxiety and resistance, and although they are generally polite, an underlying sense of hostility. Anthony Storr (1979) refers to three Hs in connection with depression: Hopeless, Helpless and Hostile. He believes that patients may not be quite as helpless as they appear. Very few of the patients have chosen to come to the group; most have been encouraged and even cajoled by the day hospital staff to do so. I'm greeted by cries of 'I can't draw', 'I'm no good at this sort of thing', 'I can't see the point of it', 'It's not what I like to do'. I reassure them that there will be no judgement or evaluation of their work, that they are being offered space that they can use for themselves.

Perhaps as I have received their leaden heaviness, so they, in turn may take from me the confidence I have gained through years of working as an art therapist. I know that the process works and, once people have access to the materials, they find they can use them. At the end of the session they are often quite surprised at what they have been able to do. There is a good variety of materials available - paint, crayons, even clay - but because of the limited space, crayons are the most frequently used.

The structure of the group is very simple. I work in a non-directive way, but usually offer a theme which is so open-ended that it can be taken in many different ways, or I may tell a short fairy story or myth. After the working period, there is a little time left to share the pictures, this is a way of helping these very isolated people to become more aware of each other. It is a gentle, nurturing group, where seeds can be sown, and through allowing things to happen freely, new attitudes may be born. If given the space in which to work, I believe the psyche has remarkable powers of healing.

The art therapy group offers patients space - just to be. There is no pressure or expectation of what they should be doing or how they should do it. They allow themselves to be open to the experience and to its possibilities; it can be a very precious space and one that is quite rare in psychiatric treatment. It takes some patients time to realise that there is no evaluation or judgement of their work - depressive people can be quite crippled by their internal figures of judgement. They worry that what they do will not be good enough and they find it hard to make decisions, for fear of making the wrong one. They often set themselves unrealistic goals which are quite impossible to achieve, thus setting themselves up for failure. They can worry so much that they are unable to make any move at all. When working in the group, their fears and anxieties are clearly apparent.

It may be a chance happening that can make a change. For example, Anna, a young girl, quite 'punk', had had more than her fair share of unhappiness throughout her life - she was now in trouble through drugs and alcohol. In common with many other young people, she liked to work with very sharp, hard pencils or felt-tip pens and set herself very high standards, expecting her images to be quite perfect. She was usually dissatisfied with her results, frequently crossing them out and starting afresh on new paper, or just saying 'I'm no good'. One week we were working on a theme of water - Anna began to 'paint' with clear water on to her paper, knowing that when it was dry there would be no trace of her work, rather confirming her opinion that there was no point in her existence. Suddenly she lifted the paper and looked at it against the light from the window. The effect was dramatic the paper appeared dark, but where she had painted in water it shone brightly with a myriad of cell-like patterns. She was very excited and had to share her experience; at the end of the session she realised that it really didn't matter what she did, that she could work freely. In subsequent sessions she worked in charcoal in a very individual way - if she made a 'mistake' she would smudge it and allow the image to alter the mistake. She gradually became increasingly spontaneous, began to accept and occasionally value what she did, at the same time becoming more approachable.

When conscious control is relaxed it is possible for feelings, which may have been pressed down into a hard block for many years, to surface; there will be feelings of loss, rejection, resentment, inferiority and of anger and hostility. These feelings have been pushed out of the way because they might inflict hurt on others; they are not 'nice'. Niceness is a quality that pervades this group - so much energy is used to keep things presentable, when underneath it is a confusing horrid mess. There is fear that some of the mess might ooze out and contaminate those around them. The art materials are excellent vehicles for expressing feelings; crayons can be worked vigorously in scribbling movements, making use of the whole arm, bringing the body into action with the mind. Paint freely allows mess - in this group it is so important that patients discover that it is safe to make a mess, which can be contained and even accepted. Often they find that this is exciting and dramatic, and they discover a totally new way of working.

In this particular group, though feelings do surface and are expressed, it is the recognition of how feelings are suppressed that is most relevant. When looking at the pictures, the patients begin to feel for those images that are oppressed, smothered, pushed on one side, and not given enough space. They notice the qualities of 'grinning and bearing it', and 'putting on a brave face'. As they work, they begin to experience for themselves the results of suppressing feelings.

Example: a woman started to draw strong denticulated images in black, red and yellow crayons - they appeared sharp and violent - then she relentlessly covered the whole drawing with grey and blue crayons until the sharp images had been completely submerged. On finishing she said 'I'm sorry, I haven't enjoyed it today'. This is a very typical comment; patients feel that they should please the therapist and that they have let them down if they haven't enjoyed the work. It is usually a relief when I say they don't have to enjoy themselves, but ask how they had actually experienced the time. This woman connected the experience to being very angry with her husband, how she had swallowed the anger and then felt abysmally miserable and let down, just as she did on completing her picture.

As patients find they have a safe channel for releasing feelings, especially those of anger and hostility, so their experience of themselves is strengthened. As a child in play, they begin to explore their boundaries, discovering how far they can go, what will happen if they do this or that, experimenting and taking chances. Some people find great enjoyment in mixing new colours with paint and find pleasure in the effect of one colour against another. They may discover how limited and restricted their life has been. A woman realised with horror that she had painted over the edge of her painting and had made a mess on the table - 'I've gone over the edge - I've gone too far.' These statements struck a chord in her - she had never been allowed to make a mess as a child and her adult life had also been kept tight, within strict boundaries.

Gradually, patients begin to accept and value what they do and, as they do so, they value and accept themselves as people. They find that it is possible to make moves on their own behalf. For example: a woman sat with her left elbow on the table, her chin cradled in her hand. Lethargically she drew horizontal lines across the paper. She had done this in previous sessions - making patterns, filling in between the lines, feeling that she was hemmed in with no means to manoeuvre. On this particular day she stopped in her tracks - her eyes widened and suddenly she turned the paper over and began to work with considerable intensity on a landscape which I felt was a landscape of her 'self'. It was a very personal picture - she had never done anything like it before and she was satisfied with the result. She said, 'I suddenly realised that I didn't have to go on in the same boring way. I could do something about it, and I did'.

John's Work

I should like to illustrate some of the points I have been making with the work of 'John', who came to sixteen sessions in the day hospital group. I knew very little about John himself; I rarely have much information about the patients in the group. John was an intelligent young man who had been a teacher and had been very successful in his work. Much of his work had been quite creative and John had found to his horror that, in his depression, the activities which had previously given him so much pleasure and fulfilment had seemingly turned against him and abandoned him. He had a very one-sided attitude, the thinking in his head dominating at the expense of his feelings. He appeared heavy, pale and listless.

In the first session John worked in charcoal and was quite surprised to be able to do anything at all. This allowed him to come to the second session with some confidence. He worked in oil pastels and produced the powerful images illustrated in *figure 3.1*. Even in black and white, we can experience the menacing power of the right-hand image - under the black lines are red and blue ones. These colours were important in the later work. The left image is much more frail; it is green in colour and looks like a pen nib. John was a writer.

Figure 3.1 - John's second session

Figure 3.2 - The Eye of Judgement

Figure 3.3 - Moving Images

Figure 3.4 - The Island

The picture contains two quite dissimilar areas which are separated and are not relating. John's own association with the right-hand image was of a powerful monster bird that threatened him; he developed this to an idea of a parrot - parrots repeat what is said to them, or only say what people want to hear. The strong eye recurred in subsequent pictures - perhaps the eye of judgement (*figure 3.2*).

In the following weeks John's images continued to express the idea of trapped energy through using bright colours encased in strong black lines, often detached and floating in space. Sometimes the images combined two ideas, for example, one appeared as a bird and a fish.

One session acted as a turning-point for John. He arrived looking very grey and lifeless and shared the utter misery of the way that the depression appeared to have sapped all his energy, leaving him with nothing at all. I suggested that the group stayed with their feelings, drawing when they felt ready to do so. John began to work listlessly, just letting the crayons move slowly across the paper. Gradually the work gathered in momentum and the finished image amazed John. It was as if a fantastic dog-like creature was leaping across the world, almost like Cerberus coming out of hell. John himself was lifted in his mood and decided to take the picture home. After this session he began to use paint.

For his first painting, John tried a 'proper' landscape. He found that it was difficult to keep with the landscape, as other ideas kept flooding in, demanding expression. He found the whole experience quite uncomfortable. In subsequent sessions he imposed a discipline on himself by restricting his colours to black, blue, red and white, which he felt would stop him painting 'nice' pictures. This says something about the way that John took control of himself. The 'discipline' did work - possibly because John wanted it to; interestingly, he had chosen the colours of the right-hand image of the second picture.

Figure 3.3 was the third picture that John painted. It is full of energy, the images were constantly changing, there were a number of images under the final picture, and if there had been more time, it is likely that the picture would have gone on moving. Such movement and change was quite a vital experience for John who had experienced himself as being so listless and resistant to change. In this picture it appears as though the right and left images are almost connected. Looking back to the picture of the second session it is clear that movement is taking place.

Figure 3.4: After painting for a number of weeks, John used crayons once again. He found his experience of them quite changed. He made a representational drawing - the theme for the group had been an island. John

Figure 3.5 - Personal Landscape

encountered considerable conflict in drawing his island. He felt that he was looking out from the centre of the island, as if from the unexplored interior. There is a very sensitively drawn hill. John's difficulty sprung from what he intended to be slender grasses blowing gently with the wind. He found himself constantly returning to work on the grasses which appeared to gather in strength and intensity. He tried to resist their power as he did not want the grasses to dominate the hill. However, in the finished picture the grasses tower above the hill in quite a definite way.

Figure 3.5 was done in the last session and John relaxed his rule over his palette, allowing himself green, blue, yellow, brown and white, and omitting the black and red. This picture appears as a landscape, a very different one from the earlier attempt. It can be viewed as a landscape of the self - there are fields, some ploughed ready for planting, others already planted - there are wild uncultivated areas and on the left-hand side there are some seed-like images which give an indication of potential growth. Through the centre of the picture, water is attempting to flow - at times a trickle, as if searching for a channel.

As the sessions progressed, John was able to release a considerable amount of energy. He made very good use of the media, both crayons and paint, and as the sessions came to a close, John's work was flowing quite freely. John stopped coming to the sessions because he was discharged from the day hospital.

When I spoke to John to ask permission to use his pictures he told me that he had found benefit in the art therapy sessions. He realised from the first session that there was no expectation of performance and this enabled him to work quite freely, allowing things to happen which had quite surprised him. He felt that something had stirred within him; that it was very special, that it belonged to him, that no-one could take it from him. He did not know quite how it would relate to his present life, but felt that in a year or two he would have a greater understanding of what had occurred. When I invited him to the Outward-Bound Group his reply was typical of many, that he felt that he was almost back to normal, that soon he would be back at work and hoped to be too busy for any group. We left it open, that he could come if he felt the need. Perhaps he now needed space on his own to let things develop.

One of the great rewards of working with this client group is the way people gradually come out of their isolation and begin to bond together and form a group. It is a magical experience. When this stage is reached, I find, on entering the little room, that I am met with a tremendous feeling of eager anticipation of what the session will bring. These are people who are coming alive, aware and able to express themselves with freedom. They have become sensitive and supportive of the other members of the group. It is only for a few weeks that the group is really working in this way, because the clients are then ready to be discharged from hospital. Those who are still vulnerable may stay behind to form the nucleus of the new group that is about to start.

I found it very frustrating that patients were discharged from hospital, ready to take up the responsibility of living their own lives, at the point in the art therapy group when it appeared that they were just beginning to stir. As they became more confident in using the art media to communicate and express their feelings, they were more prepared to look at themselves and I felt that they needed more time, but not hospital time. I was concerned that if some were not given the time and space to continue exploring their inner worlds they would need to come back into hospital. At this stage people need to be able to look at themselves from a state of 'wellness', which allows them the confidence to take on the work, rather than attempt it when they are struggling to emerge from under the shadow of illness. Thus the Outward-Bound Group was born.

The Outward-Bound Group

The Outward-Bound Group takes place in a building used for community activities. It is encouraged and well supported by the hospital authorities, who pay the rent for the room. The group has a similar structure to the one in the day hospital, but it has more space, both in terms of size and physical amenity.

A major difference between the two groups is that people come to the Outward-Bound Group because they want to. It matters to them that they come, and they give considerable commitment to the group. They can use the group for as long as they need; it may be a few months, a year, or longer. It depends on each individual. The people who attend the group come from different backgrounds and experiences of mental illness. Some follow up their work in the day hospital, others may not have been in hospital but are referred by GPs, community psychiatric nurses and social workers. There are those who have had many years' experience of long-term mental illnesses such as schizophrenia or manic depression. The group is very resilient, tolerant and accepting, and works without judgement. There is considerable trust to be found at its core. A number of people have now used the group in making their own personal journeys.

The way the group works is described by Gwen, a member of the group.

'Since experiencing art therapy during the past six or seven months I have gradually come to understand its value, particularly for people who have emotional, mental or even spiritual problems. Previously, I knew little about art therapy and understood nothing about its purpose.

The time spent at the beginning of the session, talking about problems or happenings that any of the group want to bring up, is very useful. It helps us to be aware of the difficulties and struggles that other people have, so that it puts our own thoughts and feelings into a true perspective. The art therapy then becomes important because it helps us to express our innermost thoughts through the picture without realising what is happening. Many people find it difficult to express their feelings verbally in an articulate way and possibly feel foolish or embarrassed at saying things that are very personal. The pictures we make help us to relax and perhaps even return to childhood with a simple and honest outlook on life.

I like the time to be very quiet when we are working on our pictures. That time of quietness is very important to me because I think it allows one to get in touch with thoughts and feelings from deep within. Not that I am aware of thinking anything in particular, as my mind seems to be blank as I concentrate on the picture.

One surprising thing I notice is the sense of achievement I have at the end when I produce a picture which, although it has no artistic quality, is completely personal to me. Here we can be entirely ourselves when no demands are made on us, only to be who and what we are.'

For the people who have had long experience of mental illness, the Outward-Bound Group has been of particular value. They are very controlled people, fearful of letting go and it may take a year or two before they have built up enough basic trust to allow themselves to relax and let things flow freely. In a safe, contained space, they can work quietly, using a symbolic language, allowing their story to unfold. The making of this story is healing. Art therapy is helpful because it is predominantly non-verbal and the images are constantly moving and developing. People find the support to explore the images of their inner world that has appeared to be so chaotic and threatening. As trust develops, repressed feelings begin to surface, hitherto held in place by the inner judgmental figures that are for the schizophrenic found to be mercilessly persecuting and demeaning. As these figures of judgement gradually withdraw their hold, the individual is able to develop flexibility. It has been a great joy that people have been able to use the group; initially they came, unable to communicate or express their feelings, unapproachable, distant and withdrawn, and through the group have been able to come alive and discover a real feeling of belonging. I shall now give some illustrations of clients who use the group.

Theo

I had known Theo for many years skirting around the day hospital, not being able to form any attachments apart from coming regularly to the art therapy group. He was intelligent, but had not fulfilled his potential, due to various problems which he had had from childhood. He was crippled by a chronic obsessional illness and anxiety.

He enjoyed coming to the day hospital group but needed to move into the Outward-Bound Group to be free from the pressure of time. At first he found it difficult to be in the group. Apart from myself, he rarely interacted with the other members. He made himself as obnoxious and hurtful as possible and worked on his pictures with the conscious intention of wanting to shock; often they would appear quite obscene. Over the months and years, the group kept a place for Theo, even though his attendance was erratic, due to his life being controlled by obsessional rituals. He had a wonderful collection of 1960s 78 records, of which he was very proud. His whole life revolved round these records. It was important that they were kept free from dust. If he felt that he had not been able to keep them clean, he would be in despair and spend several days in bed. Gradually Theo found that he could use the group.

One session was of particular value to him. Theo spent most of the time on a careful drawing, then, finding there was still time, started to work on another one, which was unusual, as he tended to only work on one drawing. He was relaxed and working quite freely. The group responded to the second drawing as it was very different from what they had seen before. It was sensitive and very beautiful. Theo was surprised, as he had let it happen without thinking about it. In the following session, Theo shared with the group how much the previous session had meant to him. He felt truly accepted, valued, for the first time in his life. It was a momentous experience for him that no-one could take away. He shared how he had always perceived himself as something to be despised, and had behaved in an outrageous way so that others would quickly reach a correct assessment of him. Now, he no longer needed to put on an act with the group; he could be himself. Since that time, Theo has been able to make much greater use of the group, interacting with the others, sharing his experiences and feelings and being able to listen. Recently, Chris joined the group. He too, had had years of illness and at first found it very hard to settle. It was Theo who helped him. For some it may take a long time to feel accepted, yet when it does happen, it enables the individual to grow emotionally.

Sandra

Sandra had become very depressed, following the death of her husband. She had been in the day hospital group and had been pleased to continue to work in the Outward-Bound group. In the session in which Theo shared his feelings of value, Sandra drew a lion in a cage at the zoo. She felt many people would look at this lion with wonder and awe. It was of much greater value than she herself, whom no-one ever noticed. She might just as well not exist.

Sandra was talented artistically, but had never felt good enough to make the most of her potential. She often used images of making pots out of clay, and in one session she drew the process of centring the clay on the wheel. Nearing the end of her time in the group, she drew a number of pots of interesting shapes and design. She spoke of how she wanted to work in a more creative way and of the obstacles that impeded her, mainly the voices that told her she was no good but which she was now more able to confront. A month or two after she had left the group she came back for a session. She brought with her a magnificent pot that she had made. It was tall, an exciting shape and beautifully decorated. She wanted to share with the group that the pot now existed in reality and that she was proud to own it.

Penny

Penny is a young girl, who, from early childhood had felt herself to be weird, a misfit, not belonging anywhere. While working in the group she has matured and is discovering who she is, and that life holds great possibilities for her. She makes these comments about her experience in art therapy.

> 'Art therapy - it can be said that art therapy is the draining of thoughts and feelings from the most probably worked or overworked brain or imagery of the hallucinatory mind. All the time I have been doing art therapy, I have found that I am much better with my thoughts and feelings out, rather than like being bottled up in a wine jar ready to explode. This keeps away violent behaviour. Looking at it straightforward, somehow I may have cured myself of this potent mixture of emotions, which I cannot express. Art therapy is the art in which feelings and thoughts intermingle like spaghetti and are straightened out only by painting and talking.'

The Outward-Bound Group has been going for over four years. It took time for people to recognise its potential. It is now being used well. It is valued as an 'outpost' of the day hospital, a place where people are able to continue the work started there. People are being referred who have not been in the psychiatric hospital, and this can prevent the development of more serious problems. It also offers valuable space for those people who have suffered years of illness and who gain benefit from the interaction with other members.

In coming to art therapy people discover in themselves a power to use in their own healing. They are able to take an active role in their treatment, thus raising their self-esteem and finding that they can take greater responsibility for their actions. They find a place in which to be, to discover and explore their own potential and find that they can begin to live lives that are meaningful, healthy and creative.

Chapter 4

A Place to Be

Art Therapy and Community-Based Rehabilitation

Sarah Lewis

This chapter provides a description of art therapy in a community-based, psychiatric rehabilitation service with members of long term sufferers in the population.

Rehabilitation

I take the term 'rehabilitation' to mean a process which facilitates the optimum level of functioning for a person. In the psychiatric services, the term rehabilitation is usually applied to the long term sufferers in the population. It pertains to the notion of 'resumation' of everyday life, but in an adaptive, new way, and in a way which is appropriate to each individual.

The term could equally be applied to those recently discharged from acute wards and day care facilities, where a shorter term description of the concept would perhaps more aptly be that of the 'restoration' of individuals to their ordinary lives through the working-through of feelings and difficulties.

It is the former group that I am concerned with here, where, as an art therapist, the idea of working actively to bring about change is not my primary goal. My primary task is to provide a place and an opportunity for the development of the referred person's positive attributes, to minimise individual deficiencies, and to aid the enhancement of optimum levels of functioning through a form of relationship which will flourish over a long period of time.

Although I need to know the reason for a referral to art therapy, I am not overly interested in the original diagnostic label which may have been attached to an individual. Schizophrenia, for example, seems to me to be a loose, largely undefined and unhelpful label. It suggests historically at least, a 'no-hope' prognosis with poor social implications and tends to promote a negative self-image in the individual to whom it has been applied. My own attitude is that I am primarily interested in the person, secondarily in their disability.

The enhancement and encouragement of positive attributes is at the core of the philosophy of the developing rehabilitation service. A 'Constructional' positive approach through an individualised method of Goal Planning (Gloucester House, 1987) is used by key workers with people who have been recently discharged from the long stay wards of psychiatric hospital. This means that the person's strengths are always being built upon and used as ways to overcome problems and difficulties. Firstly, it is a way of teaching new skills to people who may have had a long history of being confronted with failure; secondly Goal Planning combines the assessment and treatment phases of therapy so that these two crucial components of rehabilitation are closely linked. The person is closely involved in decision-making processes and their key worker becomes a friend, helper, teacher and confidante. Key workers meet regularly with other staff in the service - community psychiatric nurses, occupational therapists, art therapists, social workers and medical staff - to ensure that close links between residential and day care facilities are maintained as the service expands.

The day-to-day philosophy which underpins future plans for the service is intended to enable people (as far as financial and personnel constraints will allow), to achieve their highest possible level of functioning and independence, whilst building and maintaining a sense of security, self-respect and individuality (Warren, 1988).

Needs

Rehabilitation relates as a process to those who are very isolated or fragile, both socially and/or inwardly, and some may enter the process fighting the system with an element of displaced anger. Some have an intense feeling of being a failure; of weakness, insecurity, shame and despair, and of dissatisfaction. They often fear rejection by others, and feel socially inadequate. Sometimes they say they have no feelings and complain of being empty inside. They describe their lives as boring, mundane and financially difficult, but above all, lonely. At the same time, many individuals find it hard to be with others. What distinguishes the majority of the people who attend the long term art therapy groups is their struggle 'to be', at ease with and within themselves, as well as their struggle to be comfortably and ordinarily with one other person.

This need 'to be' is one of several needs which the long term art therapy groups can help to meet. Needs are personal problems re-stated in positive terms. Stating something as a problem implies that the person has to stop doing something, whereas re-framing problems into needs implies that there is something to be met; something to be gained. So, instead of saying that Susan and Anthony have the problem of being uncomfortable with other people, this can be re-defined by saying that they have a need to feel at ease with others. This changes the notion that the individual is a problem person, to that of her or him being someone with particular needs regarding relationships. The institution in which the group is set has to remain capable of sharing the values of the group with regard, for example, to tolerating some kinds of behaviour upon arrival, such as the manifestation of anxiety or agitation in the reception area of the building.

Some of the specific needs art therapy can help to meet are:

— The need to concentrate on the self.

— The need to be 'listened to', heard, seen and understood.

— The need to pass time meaningfully and creatively.

— The need to have assisted emotional or personality development.

— The need to be with, to share, to belong.

— The need for contained solitude.

— The need to have vulnerability affirmed.

— The need to express unacceptable feelings and thoughts in a non-judgemental atmosphere.

— The need to test reality, to put feelings and thoughts into perspective.

— The need to be; to have true self affirmed, accepted, enhanced.

This list is composed of needs which we all have from time to time; but the last three apply particularly to the persons in the long term groups.

The meeting of these needs by the use of art therapy has an important part to play in the rehabilitation process in that it helps to cater for the person's spiritual and emotional needs through creative behaviour. It provides time and space for psychic nourishment and a form of inner reconstruction through the making of art products, which means that for a while the individual and the therapist stop focusing on symptoms, difficulties and problems. Such a way of working provides a different focus from other kinds of art therapy groups, where goals may be more problem-focused. Attending long term art therapy groups provides an opportunity for the experiences that come from within and also for those that come from outside in everyday life to be brought up for consideration. Given that the person may be undertaking other forms of care processes, or may be on some form of maintaining medication, art therapy offers an alternative language in a social context in which to articulate the indescribable, a situation in which to try to make sense of and to integrate past and present experiences.

The making of artworks in a *group* setting can provide the following:

— A reason for meeting regularly.

— A meeting which takes place 'via' the artwork rather than as a result of symptoms and difficulties.

— A place where the potential for creative activity can be nurtured and developed.

— An activity which becomes ordinary and therefore sustainable over a long period of time.

— A medium for the expression of ideas, thoughts and feelings.

— A means for the communication of inner constraints which does not rely solely on verbal articulation, time or sequence.

— A social context for these inner images.

— A way of exploring and putting such images into perspective.

— An opportunity for reality-testing in discussion.

— A context within which it is acceptable to make a product which elsewhere might be laughed at, judged or criticised.

The context is important and falls into two parts. Firstly, the art product is the realised medium through which whatever is expressed or disclosed becomes visible and is held. But the art product is also an adjunct to the central aim of developing and maintaining the therapeutic relationship between the person and the art therapist in that it amplifies and enriches that relationship. This in no way belittles the role of the artwork, neither does it mean that it is of itself of less value; rather it becomes a means for enriching relationships in the group as a whole through the shared experience of the activities which brought it into being. In this way, it can be used to redirect the focus of attention away from an individual's preoccupation with their thoughts or behaviour.

Secondly, the social part of the context is concerned with the group as the holding environment for the person who participates in the making of artworks. The making of something from nothing involves taking a risk in that it makes it necessary to enter the unknown and is an essential part of learning to trust.

The maker is often acutely aware of elements in the artwork which are of personal significance, and may try hard to minimise these. Here, until a firm relationship is established between the person and the therapist, focusing on the social aspects of the activity - such as feedback from others or the sharing of satisfaction at achievement - helps to reduce associated anxiety and confirms that interpersonal boundaries will be respected until they are ready to enter into further disclosure (Donnelly, 1984).

In art therapy a person can choose to leave the more usual pressures associated with everyday living outside the door with regard to their artwork. Also, there is no culturally acceptable way to make a picture or to express oneself creatively using a visual medium. One of the features of art therapy which is particularly constructive for members of these groups is that it helps to increase the degree of active participation that the person undertakes in the on-going process of 'becoming'. It allows for the possibility of the individual being more in control and of being able to influence the direction of their own life more independently. People decide for themselves whether to attend a particular session, whether to use the art materials, to make an object or not; and whether to disclose associated thoughts and feelings. There are choices to be made about whether to imagine, drawing from within, or whether to work from exterior references, maybe to copy; also, whether to spend ten minutes or ten sessions on the same artwork, and which materials to use - the choices and decisions are numerous. All these, and the social factors, offer enablement and encouragement of autonomous functioning within each session, and rehearsal and reinforcement for life beyond the groups.

The Place and the People

Gloucester House is the purpose built, community base for the health district's adult psychiatric service which gave rise to the initiative for this chapter on art therapy. For effective delivery of care, the district is divided into three sectors - north, middle and south, based upon GP practices, and Gloucester House is located in the middle sector of the district. Each sector has medical staff headed by a consultant psychiatrist (two each in the northern and southern sectors). In addition to medical staff and a social worker, each sector has four community psychiatric nurses, an occupational therapist, and an art therapist who all share a sector office and make up the basic sector care team. Clinical psychologists have an input into these multi-professional teams, but as a department have not sectorised their service. There is a day care unit at Gloucester House which takes referrals from all the sectors, and day care is also now being offered as a pilot scheme in a satellite unit in each of the three sectors on one day a week. Both the departments of art therapy and occupational therapy for the psychiatric service are based at Gloucester House.

In the community-based rehabilitation service, which is not sectorised at present, the strategy is to develop art therapy groups over the whole district, although we also see people individually. Some of the groups function in a planned way, some on a drop-in basis, and this work is shared between colleagues in the department of art therapy. Our aim is to be able to make the art therapy service we offer as accessible as possible, delivering it to where people are as part of our philosophy of trying to meet needs as far as possible. It means that we stand a better chance of working effectively where and with whom we are most needed, and is the approach we take to our work in the rehabilitation service. The people attending the two art therapy groups described here attend on an out-patient basis, referrals coming from consultants, members of the teams, and also from GPs.

Because of the geographical nature of the health district, there are three long-term art therapy groups which are held at Gloucester House. They meet for two hours on Monday and Wednesday afternoons and on Friday mornings in the same reserved and purposely arranged rooms. We are concerned here with the Monday and Friday groups, although two people in the Friday group attend the other group on Wednesdays, and three people in the Monday group attend the Friday group. There are seven people in each of the Monday and Friday groups, (all men in the Monday group, and one woman and six men in the Friday group), so that altogether eleven people are involved. A maximum of eight people can be accommodated in each group, which helps to ensure that at least four individuals attend each session. In reality, the average attendance is between five and six in each group. The distribution of the eleven people in the two groups provides a range of social conditions and experience, and is thus:

Monday afternoons	**Friday mornings**
Ben, Kim, Anthony,	Kevin, Michael, Anthony
Richard, Patrick,	Richard, Patrick,
Gregory, David	Susan, Simon

Three of the eleven are married; the other eight people have remained single. The youngest person is 24, the oldest approximately 65 years old. (I say approximately, because there is no record of Ben's birthdate despite various searches made some years ago, so his age can only be 'guestimated'.)

Kim (47), David (31) and Susan (36) all live in a Training Hostel which was purchased by the health authority to house ten people for approximately two years after being discharged from the long-stay wards. When they are ready, people can move into newly-purchased group homes where they live more independently. Anthony (43) lives in a group home, and Ben in a privately rented bed-sit. Richard (34), Michael (35) and Simon (55) are the married people in the groups and live at home with their partners. Patrick (24) and Gregory (36) live at home with their parents as does Kevin (39), who has just been allocated a council flat and is preparing with some trepidation to live on his own for the first time.

All but one person have had one or a number of acute psychotic episodes and hospitalisations. The exception is Simon who was referred for art therapy by his GP following an accident which partially paralysed him, affected his speech, and left him with quite severe depression. He is disabled in a very different kind of way from the other group members, but his disablement is also long term, and his presence has benefited everyone by widening their perspectives. He has a remarkable relationship with Michael and in particular with Richard who, like Simon, is prone to depression and despair, and has also had a speech problem.

Patrick, the newest member of the groups, is the only one with employment, working part-time for the Post Office. Until fairly recently Gregory worked as a driver on the community programme, but has not found employment since this ended. Anthony, Richard, Ben and Gregory had been attending the art therapy groups for many years before my involvement with them.

Although we meet in a group situation, people remain very much individuals within that setting. This may seem an obvious thing to say, but I feel it is an important thing to emphasise. The preservation and enhancement of the personal dignity of each person must somehow remain paramount over long periods of time.

A Way to Be

Art therapy, like all forms of psychotherapy, is based upon the formation of a therapeutic alliance where the client and the therapist join in a process in the pursuit of an agreed aim. Long term sufferers in the population are not usually considered able to undertake formal psychotherapy, particularly because of their apparent inability to establish the degree of trust necessary to develop a therapeutic alliance. The broad outline of the psychotherapeutic process is the establishment of a relationship of trust, communication in words leading to some form of understanding, and eventual integration of that understanding. For this group of the population, the initial difficulty is in creating and fostering the circumstances where such a relationship can flourish. It can be entered into, but it takes much longer than is usually considered reasonable for the therapist to continue trying (Donnelly, 1988). This means that a modified approach is necessary.

There are two concepts which I have found especially helpful during the time I have been working with people in these groups. The first is that of having as a goal 'No Goal' (Donnelly, 1988). This derives neither from indifference nor inactiveness on my part. It is, rather, a means whereby an on-going space for relationships to develop can be created without time limits, so that work is, as much as is possible, in the 'present tense' every time the group meets. This makes it more possible to be able to go on meeting. Time can be passed in the groups getting to know each other appropriately and forming understandings. It also relieves the therapist of the role of the person who stands for authority, directiveness, the one who knows the answers, the one who is healthy and competent.

This brings me to the second helpful concept, very much allied to the first: that of 'Actively Doing Nothing' (Donnelly, 1988). This means not taking over, organising, getting, offering ideas and suggestions. The therapist-client relationship needs to be fostered as much as possible on a 'side-by-side' basis, especially in this situation, to survive the long term nature of it (Greenwood and Layton, 1987). However this is not a factor which can be relied upon to be assumed or accepted by people in these groups. In my experience, it almost always has to be demonstrably apparent. It is somewhere within the realm of friendship that I work with people, based as that is upon trust, consistency, equality, autonomy, and the shared experience of the artwork and its attendant paraphernalia.

Many of the individuals in the groups have become friends. Sometimes an individual's only friends lie within one of the groups. The group can be a place where much humour and friendly banter is exchanged, albeit in defence of anxiety or peer rivalry. It is also a place where 'appropriateness' can be tried out. I have observed enormous tolerance, sensitivity and awareness of others' difficulties in the jungle of what is or is not appropriate in behaviour and in the disclosure of thoughts, ideas and feelings. This is an area full of potential pitfalls: What *is* appropriate for a particular person? What *is* his or her usual self, their optimum level of functioning at any given time? Cultural norms and social mores vary greatly from person to person in these groups. Strong feelings are often expressed, particularly despair, projected aggression, or paranoid, fearful ideas. Although these are not necessarily explored, they are an express-ion of needs which require to be met and contained. Group dynamics are low-key as far as possible, maintained at the level of consciousness; the problems of everyday living are burdensome enough for most people. Low-key dynamics also help to reduce levels of anxiety in the person, making on-going attendance more possible, especially where ego boundaries may be diffuse or fragile.

One of the major problems of working with some people is often apparent at the initial phase and can recur during other phases; this is a lack of personal motivation in a referred person. The 'culture of the group' assists in meeting a motivational need, especially during the initial phase, when group members are encouraged to join with the newcomer so that the group becomes the focus of the new person's attention. This further encourages people to deal primarily with each other rather than with the therapist, the setting or the organisation. Neither the therapist nor the organisation has expectations about how the person 'should' be. As little cause as possible is given for the person to find external reasons which might prevent negative, inner feelings or thoughts from being addressed in the environment of the groups. However, if a newly referred person won't attend a first group appointment after a number of offers have been accepted by them but not taken up, it is questionable as to whether they should be pursued, and if so, for how long. We encourage the person to be responsible as far as possible for their own well-being, and also to persuade their relatives of the benefits of this.

As I indicated earlier, the groups provide a social context, a place where the individual can belong and seek support. The provision of a safe space with clear boundaries of specific times on specific days in a place which group members can call their own and which will not be intruded upon, is one of my most basic tasks. Along with this goes the preparation for each session, paying attention to the environment itself, including ordinary things like making sure that the plants are watered and the tables clean. The two adjoining rooms are prepared in advance of each session, and the materials and on-going artwork are laid out. Music is played when the session is due to start, and there are the makings for people to help themselves to tea and coffee. All this might sound pretty basic and mundane, but by these means an indication is given to the group members that the space is ready for them. Demonstrating care for the group environment may also suggest to the group members that they are cared about.

Another demonstrable factor to do with boundaries is that, pertaining to personal space, some people seem to need much more than others. Each person works on their own individual artwork within the group setting, and the physical environment needs to offer choices, for some individuals to be able to feel comfortable in, for example, choosing to be in the shared space but nearer its perimeter; this also applies to verbal interaction. Part of the culture of the groups is that it's okay not to speak, not to do, not to act, but just to be there. Some members of the groups can be very verbal at times, and another of the therapist's tasks is to protect other individuals from that, maintaining a space that can meet the needs of each person as they arise.

The doing of artwork is a way of being. Where ego boundaries are diffuse and fragile, joining in the process of forming an artefact can be seen in terms of a 'framed experience', a reflection of the internal ego boundary and also a means for defining and holding on to it. In this way art therapy offers the potential for the integration of the scattered, damaged ego within the whole person. Healing through art therapy must be the art of making whole symbolically or through imagination and within the bounds of a trusting relationship.

These long term art therapy groups provide an alternative, additional means of support for those who attend them. For some, they may be the only contact a person has with the service, apart from regular visits for medication, although in the community setting, medication is more likely to be administered at the GP's surgery. The art therapist can observe mood changes, behaviour, modes of presentation, and apparent effects of medication through the artwork making process, where changes are often heralded or anticipated. The therapist is therefore able to help in the prevention of further mental deterioration by bringing this to the attention of other professional colleagues in the Care Teams. What someone chooses to depict; the mode of the work; the degree of surface flatness or lack of pictorial depth or content; the size and type of materials chosen; and the manner in which they are applied are all elements of choice which can change and which can communicate how a person is that day and through the on-going process over time.

As indicated earlier, it is these factors in the creative process which provide the means for an individual to initiate, rehearse and demonstrate their own power and control, a means which supports the facing of realities rather than collusion with the degenerative process of illness.

The examples of the art products of a few of the people in the long term groups shown now are reflections of inner worlds; but it is important to point out that they are seen here outside the context of art therapy as a process. Some people work on the same artwork over a long period of time, are painstaking, careful, precise, and demonstrate enormous self-discipline and purpose. Michael spent twelve sessions on his 'Volcano' picture (*figure 4.1*). During the eighth session, after he had completed the painting of the volcano, he put

Figure 4.1 - Volcano

Figure 4.2 - Island

himself into the painting 'out of danger, on the path' in the foreground. He has difficulty coping with his underlying aggressive feelings, and is afraid of losing control as a result of interpersonal conflicts. Michael was diagnosed as suffering from schizophrenia at the age of 22. He is insecure in relationships, is now in his third marriage, and complains of lacking confidence, of poor concentration, and difficulty in completing tasks once started. When he had finished his 'Volcano' painting, he reflected on 'the feeling of freedom' it gave him, having been able to express aggression in a manner which was acceptable to him and over which he had had control. He also stated that he was pleased with the way he had stayed with it and completed it.

Kevin's picture of an 'Island' viewed from the cliff edge was painted over a similar number of sessions (*figure 4.2*). He went to great pains to mix precisely the right colours, trying them out on a separate sheet of paper reserved for the purpose. The manner in which he made this picture seemed to reflect his lack of confidence and spontaneity, his tentative, fearful feelings about the problems of living, and his hypochondriacal obsessions. The image itself seems a most eloquent statement about his cut-off, inner loneliness and his difficulty in relating to others. He said that he would have been on the island if he had painted himself in his picture, and he too expressed satisfaction at his achievement. His subsequent picture included two figures from the start, in the foreground of a landscape, and appeared to reflect and accompany a shift in his ability to relate to other members of the group: he had moved in from the edge.

Others may make one, two or three pictures during one session, carefully measuring the allotted time. Richard comes from a large, close-knit family who had high expectations of him as a child. He went to university at the age of 17, but became increasingly isolated and did not achieve the level of degree expected of him. He then had a failed attempt at an MSc. The onset of a major psychotic illness began when he was 22 years old, and he was subsequently admitted to psychiatric hospital. He began to have unusual movements of his face and jaw, and occluded speech (momentary closure of the vocal passage which becomes 'stopped up') which becomes worse when he is feeling stressed. At this time there appeared to be a link between his mouth problems, his feelings towards his articulate father and brother, and his fear of his 'violent and evil' thoughts about his four children. Richard has been a regular attender of the art therapy groups for four years. Both *figures 4.3* and *4.4* are representative of drawings that he makes during a single session. *Figure 4.3* is an expression of 'feeling trapped and closed in' by his circumstances, and is also a visual articulation of contained, aggressive feelings. *Figure 4.4* is an image of himself 'feeling unhappy' and wanting 'to be alone'. He added the statement

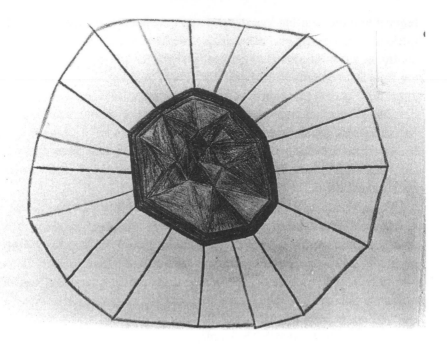

Figure 4.3 - Trapped

Figure 4.4 - Alone

'we all live like this'; a reference to his perception that others may also feel as he does.

Another person may spend ten seconds making a 'this is me right now' statement, or slightly longer on an image about themselves at the time of a particular session. Anthony has had several admissions to hospital during the past 20 years. He is constantly preoccupied with ideas about sexual relations, bodily functions and hypochondriacal symptoms which defend him against his feelings of inadequacy 'compared to real men'. He also complains of what he terms 'paranoia' which he describes as 'fluctuations in my mind'. He fears that others can tell what his thoughts are and that this will lead to violence, a projection of his own violent, aggressive ideas. His father was a commercial artist and Anthony, who has a facility for drawing, tends to compare himself unfavourably with his father's ability. *Figure 4.5* illustrates his style of drawing.

Although an accomplished drawing, the image is simple, the first lines staying unaltered, due to a degeneration of his critical faculties and to a fear of spontaneity of which he is suspicious. He has often drawn landscapes which have a magical significance for him, such as Glastonbury Tor or Stonehenge.

Figure 4.5 - Scarecrow

He says that they are 'healing places', but these images are also repetitions of those evoked in early psychotic breakdown - the most powerful, disturbing experience of his life. In *figure 4.5*, he said he added the scarecrow to the picture 'to balance it'. At the same time, it can be seen as a self-image which can be compared to that of the barren fields and the broken tree in the foreground. There are periods when Anthony does not draw at all for several sessions, needing encouragement to use the art materials. He will sit, apparently comfortable, with a previously made image of his own or one found in a book of paintings. So, although the doing and making of the artwork is important, how the person is, the being-there and being-with, is as important. The artwork gives us a subjective reason and involvement for the purpose of 'being-there-with-others'.

Sometimes someone makes an artwork with which they cannot or do not immediately acknowledge a subjective involvement. When involvement is denied or withheld it is often a communication about a feeling, perhaps an anxiety a person is experiencing at the time regarding the group, the art therapist, or themselves. It is material to be worked with and does seem to me to have to do with a problem of relatedness, to the difficulty of bringing inner, fractured or scattered elements sufficiently together. Or it may be a difficulty or fear of trying to articulate the preserved inner reality, because the space between inner and outer worlds feels too wide. Where words fail, the image can bridge that gap to some degree by taking the inside out onto the paper - making real, objectifying, enshrining and bringing together within the boundaries of the product what was held inarticulate within. Then communication in words can become possible. The unresolved issues surrounding dependency, authority, autonomy and sexuality can be faced. Insights into what they may have lost or missed in life, or may not be able to achieve, concerning work, intimate and sexual relationships, living with other people, can be talked about. They may have thoughts and feelings about life seeming to rapidly pass them by and ensuing panic, anger and despair. The art therapy groups provide a place for self expression, through which the self may be healed.

The attitude is to be as accepting of the person as straight-forwardly and as honestly as possible. If the therapist cannot cope with images, needs and questions, how is the individual to trust that the therapist will do so when they are not feeling their usual self? My experience is that both violent and sexual images are more likely to occur in acute art therapy groups, or within the bounds of an individual art therapy session than in these long term groups. The images evoked in the long term art therapy groups are usually *apparently* more superficial, more mundane and less self-aware than the images produced in other art therapy settings. They also more often evoke loneliness, isolation, recurrent inner themes, and a degree of despair related to the difficulty of living. All these features reflect the condition in which the person lives out his or her life.

The art therapy session ends with cleaning up used equipment and putting the artworks away into folders or leaving them to dry. For one or two people this may be after they have attended the two hour session for forty minutes; people are free to decide for themselves how long they stay. There are those who arrive quite early and stay right to the end - Anthony and Gregory usually do this. Ben, on the other hand arrives half an hour early and leaves half an hour before the end to go and do his shopping. Kevin invariably arrives half an hour or so after the session has begun, and then appears to have difficulty finishing his artwork and leaving - the same process that causes him to arrive late at the start of the session.

As we all set about ending, there is usually forward-looking conversation to the rest of the week or the weekend, and confirmation of our next meeting in the group. In this manner life beyond the group is faced, supported by the knowledge that the group will convene next time.

Reflections

For the art therapist, 'Actively Doing Nothing' through artwork is a way of being with people, and the long term art therapy groups are a place for people *To Be*. The on-going process of becoming through creative behaviour is fostered within a social context and a therapeutic relationship in the art therapy groups. This contributes to the rehabilitation process by offering an opportunity for the development of creative functioning for each person, based upon relationships which develop 'side-by-side' within given boundaries. Making an artwork does not depend upon verbal articulation, nor upon time or linear sequence, though that can be a manifestation of the process. For the long term groups, art therapy facilitates personal motivation, self respect, enhancement and enrichment through the autonomous functioning of the maker of artwork in a non-judgemental atmosphere, where experiences can be shared and supported. The art therapist has 'No Goal' as a goal in order to be able to be-with-others, which helps to make the work of relating with persons in the groups possible for long periods of time for both the therapist and the group members. Constancy and consistency is a formula for friendship, and is applied in a similar way to the therapeutic relationship between the therapist and long term group members. This, together with the provision of an opportunity for creative behaviour through art therapy is a way of helping the person to communicate their individual state. Having 'A Place to Be' forms part of the strategy for helping the person to be able to continue to cope with everyday life in an ordinary way during their own process of becoming.

Chapter 5

Swimming Upstream

Art Therapy with the Psychogeriatric Population in One Health District

Karen L Drucker

In this chapter I will be talking about the psychogeriatric day hospitals where I work, and will mention other facilities offered to the older population 'in psychiatric need'. By this term, I mean those people who are feeling depressed, those suffering from an anxiety and those people suffering from mild confusion. Here I will not consider people suffering from dementia, because that would need another chapter to describe a different way of working. I will look at other professional workers' attitudes toward art therapy. Following on from that, I will focus in on one woman's experience in art therapy and, finally, look at an art therapy group experience.

The Techniques

Dr I H Mian, Consultant Psychogeriatrician in Southmead Health District has stated:

> The philosophy of the service is (Mian,1985):
>
>> a) early skilled assessment at home
>> b) a multidisciplinary team approach
>> c) liaison with other services
>> d) support to relatives and other professional groups
>> e) involvement of community and voluntary groups

    f) teaching and changing the attitude of the public and profes-
        sional staff

    g) research

As an art therapist in a health district, I had been covering three day hospitals:
Dorian Day Hospital, Severnview Day Hospital and Riverside Day Hospital
for the elderly mentally ill, working both individually and in a group capacity.
I now work in Riverside Day Hospital, on in-patient Q Ward, and run an
out-patient group for community support. My skills are now concentrated on
working with those people diagnosed with depression and grief reactions and
I have requested referrals for this population. Art therapy has been beneficially
used to focus on reminiscing, life review and the positive/negative aspects of
present life situations.

    Both in the individual and group sessions, warm-up exercises are needed
to help people focus attention, and in the case of the group, to unify it into a
group activity. Techniques such as 'Pass the paper' and 'Complete the squiggle'
are a few ways of getting started. 'Pass the paper' is useful in that nobody owns
that picture and therefore would find it difficult to make a judgement on it
(*figure 5.1*).

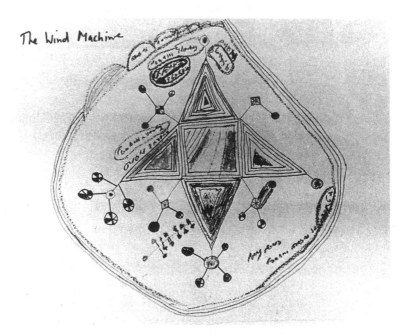

Figure 5.1 - Pass the paper: The Wind Machine

I ask people to draw something, either a design or a recognisable picture, and then after ten minutes, I ask people to pass the picture to the person on their right. The next person then adds to the picture in front of them and this continues until each person finds that he/she has the original picture. The squiggle drawing helps people get going because there is already a mark on the paper. I draw a curved line on each paper (all different curves) and ask people to make a picture from it. The images made are then looked at and discussed. Even something as simple as 'Writing Your Name' in different styles can be a good introduction, as many people feel more comfortable with writing and can expand creatively in this warm-up.

Usually group themes that arise are continued from the previous week, such as 'Wedding', 'Children', 'Family Tree' or, for sensory awareness, collages with colour, texture and smell. Using art on an individual basis needs a less structured emphasis, and I encourage the person to draw specific aspects of life events or try to build confidence by shared drawing with me. Many older people find artwork particularly difficult to participate in, because it was an activity that their children did, and they have therefore said that it felt 'childish'. Sometimes they feel that art is used to see if they are 'daft', because they know that their memories are failing and their artwork might confirm these fears. Some also associate the psychologist's testing with art therapy. However, others find artwork a useful outlet for opportunities missed in lives that had to be practical, and where there was no room for 'expressiveness' and things such as 'personal growth'. As mentioned before, people of this age group need to reminisce; to make sense of their past life events.

The Day Hospitals

The Riverside Unit, in the southern sector of the health district, was opened in 1979 for the assessment and treatment of those with 'functional complaints' and for those suffering from dementia. 'Functional complaints' are depression caused by bereavement or loss, paranoid states and neuroses. The unit has sixteen places for people from the community and nine places for patients from the assessment ward. The average length of stay is a month, although the majority of clients stay longer.

Dorian Day Hospital, in the middle sector, is the newest of the day hospitals and was opened in October 1984. It provides all facilities for assessment and treatment and has about twenty patients a day.

Severnview Day Hospital was opened in 1981 for assessment and treatment in the northern sector of the health district. Initially, it had twelve places, but this was reduced to six, and the day hospital has an in-patient ward attached.

The clients attending the day hospitals can attend either two or three days, and during each day will be included in group and individual activities. Groups include reminiscence groups, exercise, cooking, music, quizzes, discussion, grief work and current affairs. Art therapy groups are included as one of the weekly groups and there is also individual art therapy for one morning or one afternoon per week.

Most of the people in the art therapy groups are referred because it is part of their programme or because they are suffering from a 'functional complaint'. Many of the day hospitals have a mixture of people suffering from 'functional complaints' as well as dementia and I thought it more appropriate to work with those people who were not suffering mainly from dementia. I found, in my past experience, that people suffering from severe dementia could not concentrate for any period of time, found it difficult to manipulate the art materials, could not relate to any theme about themselves or the other clients around them. People suffering from functional disorders (including having some mild dementia) are able to do the above (with exceptions) and are therefore able to reflect and bring about change for themselves (even if minimally!). They may even come to the conclusion that there is no possibility for change. The members of the teams in each of these day hospitals comprise the nursing staff, occupational therapy staff, physiotherapist, dietician, psychologist, social worker, medical consultant, clinical assistant, clerical, transport, domestic staff and volunteers. There are many other agencies that are involved in working with the elderly in the health district and I won't begin to try and name them all.

I was involved in the beginnings of the Trefgarne Initiative, a day pilot scheme set up by the joint funding of social services and the health authority. This scheme enabled older people with senile dementia to benefit from being involved in social and creative activities and again, art therapy was one of these. In 1977, SEMI (Support for the Elderly Mentally Infirm) was started to support relatives and carers by running a sitting service and by setting up day centres. In addition, the health district has many day centres held in elderly persons' dwellings, run by occupational therapists and community psychiatric nurses backed up by other staff and volunteers.

I continue to run an outpatient art therapy group for older people one morning a week, held in the art therapy department of Gloucester House, which is an out-patient, adult psychiatric facility. The people who attend this group are referred by day hospital staff, or by community psychiatric nurses, psycho-logists, GPs and other professionals in the district. The members of the group are those who need a safe environment to be 'creative', and who need the social support after leaving the day hospitals. The group also forms a 'surrogate family' of six to eight people who can share the similar interest of artwork in a non-threatening, encouraging way. This outpatient group is a separate group from the day hospitals, although people are referred from the day hospitals after they are discharged from them. Sometimes, people from this group need to be readmitted to one of the day hospitals, and in those cases will be attending the out-patient art therapy group at the same time as attending the day hospital.

Attitudes to Old Age

At this point I would like to comment on 'teaching and changing the attitude of the public and professional staff' (listed under Dr. Mian's philosophy of service at the beginning of the chapter). When I first started working with 'older people', during my art therapy training, I can remember several people on my course saying very firmly, 'I could never work with the elderly - that population is not interesting enough'. I remember thinking at the time, 'Not interesting enough? - people who have been through two world wars, raised families, experienced many varieties of employment, seen technology develop, felt pain and happiness, love and envy longer than I have, must have something going for them!' I had missed experiencing my own grandparents as they had died before I was born, and I was intrigued by older people's extremes in character. I felt that older people were able to show anger and resentment that I was unable to show to people in authority. At the same time, they showed a dependency towards family and professionals that stirred up feelings in me of rebellion and questioning.

In the book *Psychogeriatrics - An Introduction to the Psychiatry of Old Age*, Brice Pitt (Pitt 1982) lists the following harmful, ageist prejudices: defeatism, domination and insularity. *Defeatism* is the attitude that, because of your age, there is an inevitable consequence, that is, 'what can you expect at your age?' Many doctors with this attitude (the 'anno domini' philosophy) withhold treatment until there is a crisis, with the result that resources tend to be misused. Sick people are admitted to elderly people's homes, and social problems are dealt with by admission to acute medical and surgical wards. The physical problems of the elderly are given higher priority than the psychological needs mainly because the physical ailments seem more treatable. Those who are not sick but who are physically infirm are sometimes misplaced into a restricted hospital setting.

Domination takes two forms: the first is a hostile, disparaging attitude: people in the healing professions sometimes seem to have a need to see people (patients) getting better, otherwise these colleagues feel worthless in themselves. I have come across many colleagues who feel this way, and their idea of an art therapy group is to 'paint pretty pictures to hang on the wall'. Their frustration of wanting clients to be happy because it indicates improvement is not always resolved by the pretty pictures. Therefore, the frustration can lead to hostility. It doesn't seem to cross their minds that these groups of older people need to be left alone, not only to paint and draw happy memories and present feelings, but more importantly to express their painful, sorrowful feelings as well. I also find it difficult to put across to other colleagues that, although sometimes people would wish their pictures to be shown, many others would be likely to want to hide or destroy what they have produced, because they themselves are feeling so hopeless.

Sentimental patronising is another destructive way of treating older people - 'They're just like children, really. Isn't she a sweet old duck?' (Pitt, 1982) This attitude deprives people of their dignity and increases dependency. I have had staff members come up to me during an art therapy session and say to a group member 'Isn't that a pretty picture, why don't you draw me a house?'

Insularity quite frequently occurs when there is a division between different workers involved in working with older people: often the right hand doesn't know what the left hand is doing. The GP, the health visitor, the meals-on-wheels organiser, the home help, the social worker, are all involved but communication between them is lacking or difficult to co-ordinate. This often leads to much duplication of care for the person. In one day hospital, when I was holding an art therapy group, I discovered that the nurses or occupational therapists were holding an art therapy group either at the same time or during another part of the day. Although the approach of their art groups was different, the lack of communication to me about these groups made me feel defensive. The differences between the two kinds of art group had also not been made clear to the older people involved. The result was that I had someone from my group asking to finish a collage that they started yesterday during the other art group!

I don't want to generalise and say that all staff have these attitudes, but in my many years of working as an art therapist, many colleagues have found art therapy for this population a difficult concept to understand despite frequent educational talks and presentations to them. There seems to be an emphasis on doing things to and with older people - rather than just letting them be and do for themselves, and allowing them to set their own pace and explore from within, even if it doesn't reach staff expectations. It was only when other staff joined in the art therapy groups that attitudes began to change. It became a two-way interchange. Sometimes a nurse or nursing assistant would be interested in becoming a co-leader of an art therapy group. I would then explain to that particular person the history of art therapy, my art therapy history (my training, my work experience). I also describe and explain the format of the group - the clients involved, what has been covered (in terms of themes) in the group so far, and what needs to be looked at. I emphasise that she/he doesn't have to be 'a good artist' and that stating this to the other members of the group would be more constructive than saying 'I'm not very good at art'. The participation of the nurse or nursing assistant and occupational therapists in the art therapy groups has helped them to get to know the clients over a consistent period of time. It has also helped them understand the process taking place within an art therapy group as well as lessening their particular fears about using art for themselves in a non-activity, non-practical basis. This participation has improved our working relationship and reduced the misunderstandings. I began to realise that other professionals such as nurses, clinical assistants, social workers etc are very much more involved in their own special areas of work and do not always have time to expand their knowledge of each others' specialities. However, I did feel as if I was 'swimming upstream' in relaying to other staff the needs of older people for more self-expression and the importance of staff acceptance of this self-expression, which did change with their participation. These expectations can compound the difficulties of some older people, who have high expectations of themselves at a time when they are not able to live up to them. Sometimes, just listening and sharing helps at this particular time.

Mrs G

While I was working at Riverside Psychogeriatric Day Hospital, an older woman was referred to me by the staff at the day hospital. Mrs G was originally referred to the day hospital when she became depressed after an eye operation. She became non-communicative to both her family and friends, would stare into space for long periods of time, and not respond to personal questions asked of her. Mrs G was given brainscans which showed no dementia and she was therefore diagnosed as depressed. My other professional colleagues could not get to grips with what approach to use and wondered if a 'non-verbal' one (combined with medication) should be tried. Art therapy seemed the most suitable because Mrs G was not communicating her distress and would continue to have no eye contact with anyone. It was brought to my attention by other staff that Mrs G's husband was interested in art, in fact he considered art as his main hobby. Because of this, I thought that Mrs G might be feeling under pressure to perform, so I constantly reminded myself to 'hold back' and let her take the initiative with support (as in most of art therapy practice). As her husband 'was the artist', I made it clear that this was her time and space with me to do what *she* wanted (or did not want) to do creatively.

My first impression was that Mrs G took care of her appearance in the way she dressed, but that she was very thin because of her loss of appetite.

At the beginning

At the beginning of the sessions, I decided to structure her hour with me by drawing a series of 'squiggles'. I found that during the first session, Mrs G was more relaxed than during the sessions that followed, an unusual state of affairs that changed only during the last few sessions. Other staff members had correlated Mrs. G's past experience of being a teacher with her being a 'perfectionist', but it is not my experience that all teachers are perfectionists. However, Mrs G did demonstrate the need to be in total control, so I went along with that need by bringing in biscuit cutters for her to trace around. She was very cautious, and careful to choose the 'right colours' and keep the 'right balance of shapes' but did decide to make four combinations of shapes, all slightly different. This picture took four weeks to complete. I then brought in a packet of coloured paper shapes which Mrs G used to make a very intricate design (*figure 5.2*).

The right side of the picture looked to me like a traffic sign emphasising the 'amber warning light', while on the left side she was beginning to let a shape peek through an opening. Mrs G began talking about her daughters and reminisced about their childhood, the first time in six weeks that she had revealed anything of her home life to me.

Taking her own initiative

After eight weeks, Mrs. G was taking on her own initiatives and decided to bring a protractor to draw her own shapes. From there, she began choosing images from magazines to make picture narratives (picture of 'Girl with Balloon'). She became fascinated with overlapping pictures and enjoyed making three dimensional effects. This led on to her talking about her past

Figure 5.2 - The Traffic Sign

Figure 5. 3 - Fish out of Water

travels abroad and hobbies she had once had, but now found too difficult to keep going (pictures of flags, boat and horses). By this time Mrs G was sharing with me her fear of being totally dependent on her husband and her fear of losing control of her health. At this point Mrs G's medication was changed and her depression was lifting at a quicker rate than before. In the 'Fish' picture, (*figure 5.3*) Mrs G said that she felt like a 'fish out of water' and shared the fact that she was too embarrassed to entertain friends as she had done in the past because of her 'illness' and her inability to be sociable.

Figure 5.4 - Magazine collage

Gaining self respect

During the eight months in the day hospital and attending art therapy, Mrs G had regained self respect. She was proud of celebrating her golden wedding anniversary and decided to make a collage of her fifty years of marriage. She even included her wedding cake decorations which were very precious to her. As Mrs G was slowly returning to some of her interests and was physically better, she was discharged from the day hospital and, at her request, I continued to see her as an outpatient. She was no longer cautious, and her eye contact was warm and humorous. When she stared into space it was because she was day-dreaming and not because she was afraid. Her magazine collage pictures were large, bold and full of energy and colour (*figure 5.4*). She decided to end the sessions before going away on holiday, and finished with a hug and 'best wishes'. When I met her husband in the reception area, he said that they were going to attempt to do water colour pictures together.

Group Art Therapy

Because each person has a different length of stay within each day hospital, I found that my groups had to remain open groups (that is, new people joined at any time). It was therefore almost impossible to see a beginning, middle and end in the group process. However, there was one group which was an exception to this - the same eight people (two men and six women) remained in the group for a period of six months consecutively. I shall not describe each individual within the group but instead how they changed within the group dynamics.

Group beginnings

At the beginning, three women in the group were interested in art and did not find it difficult to put pen to paper. The others were reluctant to do so, and were also unsure how the group would help them and what I expected from them. I tried to explain that they 'didn't have to know anything about art', that 'what they did didn't have to be great works of art', that there was no 'right' or 'wrong' in the group, and that this was 'a way of getting to know ourselves and others'. All these words fell amongst anxious faces, except for the three women (already mentioned) who thought that they were going to do pictures of flowers! I found that I needed to be directive for the first couple of sessions so that anxiety wouldn't get the better of them.

I suggested writing names in different styles, completing squiggle drawings and passing pictures to each other. These exercises seemed to help reduce their anxiety, showed that nobody can 'fail', and that everyone in their own way can be creative. Writing names in different styles gave rise to comments such as 'I usually write my name in such a small way; it is so nice to write it big and bold!' Another member stated that she missed hearing the nickname that her husband used to call her instead of her name.

The squiggle drawings also opened up talk about past memories. One woman made her squiggle into a book, saying that she could no longer concentrate to read a book as she used to do in the past. Another woman (I shall call her Mrs P) talked about her experiences in Jamaica. We all decided to make a mural about her house there. She gave instructions about its appearance and we shared in the drawing of it. In this way, Mrs P made an opportunity for other people to be more personally revealing within the group.

Several of the women talked about their fears of being moved into nursing homes and losing their own homes which they had lived in since they were married. They thought that, at some point, coping with the day-to-day running of their large houses would become impossible. One man talked about his travels in the merchant navy and how his life had changed after his return to Bristol. We looked at families (making family trees), weddings (drawing pictures of weddings), children and grandchildren, and made collages of how they felt about their lives now. One woman made a 'hotch-potch', saying that sometimes she felt disorganised. Another said that she hated staying in the house and spent most of her time walking outside, and was lonely; she used her picture to depict the opposite and celebrate.

The middle period

The group became cohesive and people in the group noticed if someone was missing. 'Where is Agnes? Is she all right?' 'The transport didn't pick Mary up - she didn't look well last week'. There was a feeling of belonging and caring. We joined in a group mural where everyone had a section of 'the pie'. I drew a large circle and divided up this circle into equal segments, one for each member of the group to paint or draw within. The directions I gave were minimal, saying they could draw or paint whatever they wished, but that everyone should contribute to the space in the middle of the picture. People sitting next to each other took notice of what each other was painting, so there was considerable merging and sharing of colours and shapes, except for the lone man who was missing his male colleague that day. He was determined to keep separate, and boldly painted the boat that he travelled on when he was in the merchant navy. We looked at the finished picture and agreed that we could keep our own identities and at the same time merge as one.

The ending of the group

Towards the end of the sessions, one member commented that it felt like being in a family together. The group was coming to a close after approximately six months. Three of the women clients were discussed at the case conference and it was decided by the team (myself included) that they needed community support (day centres) and were well enough to be discharged from the day

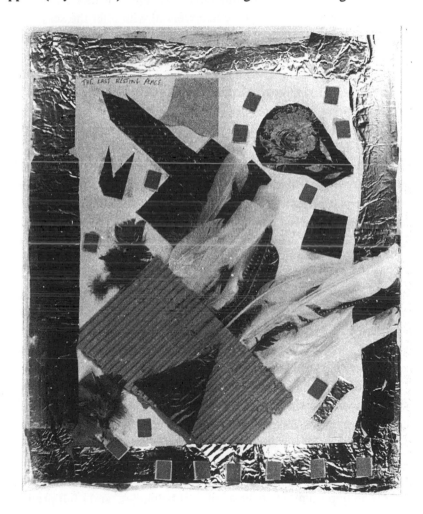

Figure 5.5 - Sharing a picture: The Last Resting Place

hospital. Another of the women members was interested in attending the out-patient art therapy group and was therefore discharged to that particular group. Because of the changes taking place, we all felt it was appropriate to end the group and that I would start a new group with new members from the day hospital. I placed three large bags of collage material onto the table and asked two people to share one piece of paper to make a picture. The two men worked together. One of them used the collage materials around the outside of the paper, making a border, while the other man worked in the central part of the picture (*figure 5.5*). The man working on the outside of the paper said that he was observing what his partner was doing and got his ideas from what was being created in the middle. He admitted to never being a leader. Most agreed that they felt closer to the person they had worked with after the session. We had an ending mural, drawing around our hands to say goodbye. I asked members what they thought about being in this type of group; not painting pretty flowers or making a picture together which looked like a 'work of art' to hang on the wall. One woman still insisted that she was 'no good at art' and that her 'grandson could do better'. But the rest said that they had relaxed more as we all got to know one another, and that it was interesting using art in a different way. I felt closer to each person and was sorry to see the group end. As mentioned before, the majority of people were being discharged to a variety of social groups. One of the women was going to the outpatient art therapy group for older people. As she walked out of the room, she turned to me and said, 'See you next week, all being well'.

Conclusion

I have found it both difficult and rewarding working with the psychogeriatric population in the Southmead Health District, and this is true both of my work with elderly people and of my liaison with other professional colleagues.

Many of the elderly people with whom I worked, felt they were 'swimming upstream' against physical illness and emotional loss. In a way, they were trying to find their 'source' - their past life events taking on new meanings as salmon swim to their source to spawn and begin new life. They were able to use the structured art therapy sessions to express their feelings, explore their difficulties about 'being old', and share together or confide in me. Getting through their resistances and insecurities about not being able to draw or paint resulted in opening up expressions of negative as well as positive feelings. It also gave these people an opportunity to have a sense of belonging, and I felt privileged to belong with them.

My feelings of 'swimming upstream' (against the flow of the water) in working with other professional colleagues in my team initially seemed a difficulty. However, this motivated me to continue to educate my colleagues about art therapy, and to evaluate continually how I was working with older clients. Gradually referrals from colleagues have increased, and have also become more appropriate.

My hope is that attitudes concerning working with the 'psychogeriatric population' will continue to change. Alongside the vital monitoring of physical illness and practical difficulties, I feel it is just as important to open up the creative 'blocks' for this age group. As this becomes more accepted, perhaps the older person and myself will not have such a long swim upstream.

Chapter 6

Art Therapy as Part of the World of Dyslexic Children

Tish Feilden

Introduction

Castleford, once a stately home of considerable beauty set in a rolling pastoral landscape, is the environment for some seventy children who suffer from specific learning difficulties. The school (Castleford is not its real name) is residential and in the independent sector, but the fees for children are paid by local authorities. I am there once a week offering an art therapy group for voluntary attendance, a place for children to focus on and explore their feelings. The only common denominator between the children is their difficulty in reading and writing. They fall into a span of ages, intelligence, communicative ability and maturity. There is an almost even split between girls and boys.

This briefly is the scene and the cast. In this chapter I wish to convey some of the drama and explore the dynamics. I describe the art therapy group that I established and share some extracts from its life. I go on to consider the relationship between myself, this form of therapy and the wider context of staff-pupil relationships.

The Art Group

My initial contact with the school was to provide psychotherapy for the few children who were failing to thrive emotionally and were showing difficulty in communicating their needs. Since the resource of individual therapy was both relatively expensive and scarce, I suggested we pilot an art therapy group where children could self select. Clearly some of the most needy children would also be the most resistant. We lived in hope, to some extent now fulfilled, that the group would establish its own identity whereby its members would encourage their peers, those that they knew to be unhappy or 'have problems', to come along and join. It was hard to know how to describe the group to its potential members. Art was associated with formal art lessons. Therapy was an unfamiliar or threatening term to most pupils. We billed the group loosely 'Self-expression through art'. To my surprise, the initial shock, 'This is not what we expected', wore off after a couple of sessions. The children came back. It was their choice. They were both open and willing to take part in emotional self-examination.

We had created our own culture. The group was to be a place that ran in parallel with the ordinary school day, offered at a time when other activities were on offer and freely chosen. We had as our venue a cottage used for extra-mural activities, thus creating a symbolic division between formal school and this group. I was an outsider. I did not belong to the 'staff'. Just as children often confide in an aunt or uncle in preference to a parent, this safe distance was created.

We set very few ground rules, but some important boundaries emerged. We needed to feel that the rules of confidentiality would be respected. Gossiping around the school about the group was out. We aimed for a climate of security, openness, informality, friendship, relaxation and support. The children were more apt to remind or point out these aspects to each other than I was. They protected their own boundaries and identity, and reminded each other when these were transgressed. They came to use the space productively. If someone appeared to be wasting their time, the reminder came from the group members. They seldom came for idle chatter and were well motivated.

We had on offer a range of art materials - clay, paper, paints, scissors, crayons. They could choose their materials and subject matter. I would suggest a theme, but this was optional. I was impressed with the intensity and absorption encouraged by the creative process. Sometimes the desired communication was quickly achieved, and its creator wished for some confidential time to share this process. The group was seldom so competitive as to prevent this. Often the individual shared long-buried secrets or faced up to previously inadmissible realities. As the children were away from home, there was a tendency to romanticise their families and their relationship with them. Although very painful, they often revealed the opposite scenario, a more authentic picture of their relationship with their families. This was experienced as the removal of quite a burden.

At first I spent my time working with individuals, engaging with the process as it emerged from sharing their pictures, clay models, scribbles, or forlorn and angry attempts at self expression. As the group gelled, more of this sharing happened in the group. Some sharing of individual stories may bring to light these processes.

Bella

Arabella is one such child. She is plump, constantly smiling, desperate to attract boys' attention, very flirtatious and, oddly inappropriate for her twelve years, dressed in young girls' clothes yet wearing make up and pouting. She has irritated the girls. They burst in, 'Bella is a terrible wind-up. She's getting on our nerves. She keeps going after the boys, flirting with them, showing herself off. Then she gets into fights and starts swearing.' I am alerted to this little girl's emotional promiscuity. She wants contact, cuddles, friendship; if that fails, arguments will do instead. Negative attention is better than none at all. She chooses to work with paint. The paper ends up as a muddy puddle. Bella screws it up and looks around. I share with her my awareness of her urge to play with the paint, how hard it is for her to produce something she likes, how she reduces it to a mess and how she is angry and fed up when destroying the image. I tell her that I am wondering if that is how she feels about herself. She nods, catches my eye for an instant and then returns to her customary scanning of everyone else in the room. 'You find it very hard to concentrate on yourself, is that right?', I ask. Another momentary glance and a nod. The smile is still fixed. 'You seem to want to please.' More smiles, nods and a little eye contact with me, but the roving attention still prevails.

I am aware of the malleability of this child. I remind myself that her assenting nature could make it easy to put words in her mouth. I offer her another chance to paint, suggesting she shares something about herself, her family, her life before coming to Castleford. She paints and draws herself and her sisters and a pony. There are several houses. I am told how her father has lots of houses. I am given the impression of wealth, an idealised picture of Bella on holiday. I am guessing, from her difficulty in describing her home, that this is possibly where her anxiety is located. Her 'sweetness' does not match up with the behaviour the other children complained of when they arrived, or her messy picture. I am beginning to form an impression of a very defended child, a child who is confused. I can sense her craving for affection. I wonder from whom she needs it most.

One day Bella arrives anxious to show me a catalogue containing horses that are offered for adoption. She explains that she wishes to adopt a horse named Belinda and shows me its picture. Belinda has been cruelly treated and then rescued and taken to the horse sanctuary. The catalogue is produced by this sanctuary in the hope of finding people willing to pay an annual fee towards the upkeep of the horse. Bella is keen for me to show an interest. I ask her what she loves about horses. She explains that they are sensitive and beautiful creatures, that they love attention and enjoy being groomed. They can also be wild and naughty. I ask Bella if she shares some of these characteristics and also ask how she feels about the horse she wishes to adopt. She says she feels like the horse in the picture, she needs rescuing. The name Belinda is obviously chosen and not coincidental.

Very gradually Bella reveals more through her own pictures and clay models. For me each one is a story, a metaphor, as is her way of approaching the creative process. In a session the day before her thirteenth birthday, she works hard at making a clay birthday cake. The care and detail she bestows on this creation is unusual. Talking to her about the importance of this birthday for her, I come to see the conflict she experiences between the part of her that wants to be grown up and a sexually attractive woman, and the other part, the very little girl that still exists inside her who craves cuddles and affection.

When she goes on to describe the birthday party she wishes to have, she manages to convey the focus of this struggle in her relationship with her father. She is not sure if she wants him to attend. I invite her to do a picture of the party. In this she conveys a sophisticated seductive image of herself. Her father is portrayed on the edge of the picture. Using this as a focus, Bella manages to express some of her ambivalence towards her father. She describes how he teases her, puts her down for her plumpness and lack of literacy skills, yet his physical attention is threatening to her. She holds some hope that her teenage self would be more lovable. Understandably, she consciously resents her father who does not meet her current needs.

I gain as much information about Bella by observing her body language, her mood on arrival, her peripheral communication to others in the group, as I do from the actual art work. I try to help her describe her feelings and amplify them, locating them in the here-and-now, in the texture of everyday life, her current and past experience. As the feelings come alive I try to respond to them as they affect me. I also encourage the group to respond, to give feedback, support her in receiving that which is confrontational and negative, and also to take in the positive (which is equally difficult for a child with a poor self image). At times I am like the advocate that Alice Miller (1979) prescribes for the damaged child. It is as if Bella cannot even recognise the hurt she feels until she knows the support is there to bear it. Like so many sad children, her behaviour is her enemy. She shows her craving for attention and affection through inappropriate and alienating behaviour. When I offer support for her to become more authentic in her feelings and express them, she can become real and available to empathic response from the group. The process is slow, and three years later Bella is still coming to the group, where we watch her grow in self confidence and allow some of the rawness of her experience of life to be shared. She is less lonely and isolated, feelings which if not negotiated in childhood can be exacerbated in adulthood.

The children are aware of each other's phony defences and they often see through each other before I do. Their cruelty is shocking at times, but if I am prepared to stay with the confrontations they offer each other, they often bear fruit.

Peter and Sara's interaction.

Peter, aged twelve, has been subject to this gruelling process. He is a good-looking boy with considerable charm, much of which is reserved for adults. He wants to tell me so much. The subject matter is usually confidential, a guarantee to gain my undivided attention. His pictures are full of his concerns about having supernatural powers. The ordinary has no place in his communication. He is full of the extra-ordinary. His feelings of being invested with special powers hold him apart from all but a very few. My feelings about his communications have shifted. At first I felt almost irritated by their obsessive nature and had great difficulty in holding back the scepticism with which I reacted to the super-natural content. I found it hard to be empathic or treat the content seriously. This child was desperate to attract my attention, but it was difficult for me to give it. Was I picking up on a counter-transference? Was our contact reproducing the feelings that exist between Peter and his parents?

Having allowed myself to pause for reflection, I felt a shift in myself and could then respond to the feelings of anxiety in Peter and become more attentive to what he was sharing with me. I fed back to him my awareness of his need to be special, his difficulty in feeling similarity to other children, his wanting and not wanting the powers that his dreams gave him. If I made the content of his work my primary focus, I was concerned about the degree of flight from reality. Sharing the de-coded messages, admittedly a process of guessing, since there is no single interpretation of images, I tried to bring the process alive in our relationship, the relationship in the group, and his relationship with his family.

Sara, aged 15, is the group member who ferociously, but ultimately crea-tively, challenged Peter's patterns. Maybe I had colluded in his one-to-one relationship with me and general lack of concern for other members of the group. He had created a privileged private world. Sara burst into this. She was angry at Peter's inappropriateness as he cut across something someone else was saying. Sara accused him of being 'a selfish creep, always asking for adult attention, ignoring other children, making out he was special.' She was bitter and unrepentant. Peter grew pink but remained silent. He refused to defend himself. I suggested that one of the other boys whom I knew Peter admired, 'double' for him, as in psychodrama (Moreno, 1969). John spoke as if he were Peter, responding to Sara, saying he felt very hurt and unsupported by all the group. Peter's silence continued. Eventually he burst through it with, 'Yes, she is right, I am a bastard, I should never have been born'. He was well into feelings of deep misery and I was reminded of his first picture, a monster figure with horns, a self-portrait labelled, 'The little tyke was born'. This had been followed by a clay model of a half monster, half devil figure. I wondered if he had picked up something doubtful about his origins? Or, was his negative self so unacceptable to himself, to his family, that he split it off and attributed it to a devil self?

Peter's over-statement and following tears allowed Sara to relax. She replied that she had never said he was a bastard, just self-centred and a creep. Her main objection was his way of manipulating staff into paying him attention, and here in the group to gaining my attention, to the detriment of others. Reflecting this back to Sara, I wondered if she was projecting some of her need to be noticed and difficulty in asking for attention.

Peter left the session accompanied by the boy I knew he liked, but whom he had never felt able to tell this. I suggested John help him integrate back into the school that evening and be sensitive to Peter's needs.

The following week Peter offered his sweets around the group, making more eye contact. This was a first. Sara was more available and less defended. I felt able to reach her. She had been a catalyst for an important confrontation, harsher than one I would precipitate, but intuitively accurate for what Peter needed. She had broken through his barrier, reduced his isolation. She had confirmed his ordinariness while giving access to her own pent-up anger. This release gave Sara the way forward to show her own vulnerability.

Linda

Linda is an attractive 15 year old girl. She presents a fairly hard image to the outer world. She appears sophisticated, quick-witted, quick to put down (and, less obviously, to be put down). Beneath the tough exterior is a small girl, desperately wanting attention, in fierce competition with her mother. She has worked with startling honesty in the group, using it as a place to access her extreme feelings of hostility towards her mother and underlying need for love. Her first picture, the story of her life, gave a simple but graphic portrayal of the pain in her relationship with her mother, jealousy of her brother, and absence of relationship with her father. The candidness of the images contrasted with the flatness of her personal presentation. I was curious. Staying with the images and not succumbing to her offhandedness, revealed rage towards her mother, and beneath this the painful conflict of longing for love.

Linda always had a close relationship with a boyfriend. She neglected peer-group relationships and potential support from other girls, presenting a tough 'devil-may-care' exterior. She seemed to arrive at sessions out of the arms of her boyfriend and return to him after sessions. Her need for comfort was great. In the group she found it harder to show her neediness, often being better at projecting this and providing comfort to others. She began to take her pictures to show her boyfriend, and within the relative safety of this relationship, explore a more authentic way of being.

Linda learnt to remove some of the tougher layers of herself and describe her neediness. She exposed the little girl beneath the cool young woman exterior, and the split became less wide. She struggled with adolescent rebellion as she encountered the boundaries of home and school. She broke rules, received sanctions, came to the group and spilt out her frustrations.

As is common to so many of us, Linda's defences served to frustrate her deeper wishes. It took her two years in the group, and some individual work, before she could begin to let go of the patterns that had taken so long to establish. Defences serve their purposes. They are often adaptive ways of coping in a world of harsh realities. Linda had to learn through trust to allow herself to experiment with giving up some of the tougher layers of her exterior. We have no way of knowing how lasting her experiences in the group will prove to be. I personally have to work in the faith that small changes are better than none at all. Feedback from young people I have met years later has helped me to realise that they seldom forget experiences that opened new horizons.

As an older and more articulate member of the group, Linda had acted as a support and catalyst for other people. I have been struck by the richness of a mixed sex and age group. There is a generosity in self-examination. Each member's openness and vulnerability gives permission to the frankness of others.

In bringing together my work as an art therapist and as a psychotherapist, I try to keep alive and validate the emotions contacted through the art work. Some individuals may need encouragement to stay with their discoveries, and support to integrate these into their lives. In the group the kind of 'games' we all play in defence of our feelings can be captured, shared, examined and maybe discarded. Group interaction is an important part of this learning, which, for the group described, then needs to be transmitted into the everyday life of the school.

Relationship Between the School and Myself

The image I have of our relationship is of two cousins meeting. We share some basic concepts. I am familiar with educational establishments for children with special needs, as I worked previously in schools for severely maladjusted children. There we worked actively with disturbance, maybe sometimes 'over-pathologising', possibly with too much investment in 'disturbance'. At Castleford the children are selected for educational rather than emotional neediness. Although the emotions are not 'centre stage', the children are nurtured, cared for holistically, and their individuality respected. The community is a caring one.

I entered this 'family', like a distant cousin, with the required minimum of familiarity. However my different origins, my label of psychotherapist, my psychological bias, and focus on therapy rather than education, can present obstacles. The resulting differences in language and cultural expectations can create a mutual wariness.

Communication was my chief concern, especially for the children to communicate and find relief from the pressure of misunderstandings, loneliness and unhappiness. However, I was unaware of how my very existence was creating another communication to staff. I was seen as an intruder and a threat. Psychotherapists can make people defensive. As a profession we use jargon amongst ourselves, and often with others. Within a common culture this may be a useful shorthand, but in a different setting it can be confusing and unhelpful. I made many mistakes in introducing my concepts to other non-psychological staff. My language and models of development, my faith in allowing the pain and its attendant behaviour to surface, (e.g. rage and anger in a previously cut-off and frozen child), and my belief in the process of making the unconscious conscious, were not always popular.

I hoped to create a secure environment, a place that could heal hurtful past experiences, to enable children to be more authentic. But this could give rise to problems for staff. Behaviour would obviously spill over into the general environment, often be disruptive, confusing, possibly out of step with the familiar. The care staff and teachers pick up the pieces at the end of the day, throughout the week, in the classroom, in leisure time. Some of the effects of

my work with children could prove to indicate in the short term more disturbance than was previously visible. This could easily produce concerns that
therapy actually causes problems.

It was hard to find a system of feedback that preserved the child's confidentiality yet gave staff an adequate emotional picture. Finding sufficient time,
contacting relevant people, highlighted the problem of all schools; how to
maintain adequate communication. Our challenge was as adults to find a
mutually trusting and respectful relationship. Without this, the split between
the staff's and my attitudes could encourage psychological splitting, ie keeping
a positive role in some relationships while hiving off the 'unacceptable' parts
of the self for other relationships. The school easily becomes a symbol for the
family. Just as children try to split their parents, ('Mum's a softy, I can walk
all over her, Dad's the one to watch out for') they could split me off from the
rest of the staff. I tried to remain conscious of these possibilities, and keep in
mind our task of enabling children to be whole and real.

Sometimes the art process was a long painful struggle, involving surfacing
pre-verbal or blocked feelings. The messiness of pictures, the blocking-out of
images and attempts of denial, repetition of content, and compulsiveness in
ways of tackling a project were all important aspects, and I tried to communicate
these to other staff where possible.

The children come to the group with issues generated elsewhere in the
school. Children who find it hard to settle to their own tasks and are more
interested in other people, may be avoiding their own emotions. Others may
bring a red-hot issue from their peer group dynamics, and then attempt to
dominate the group with hostile gossip, covering their own feelings of power-
lessness. The general chatter in the group often takes up a theme, sometimes
illuminating relationship problems that have some universality for the group.
The less confident and vocal children also have a chance to share their thoughts
and feelings.

My roles in the group were various. Sometimes the issues raised required
amplification, holding an image, story or metaphor and allowing it to develop,
to be seen from different perspectives, walked around, identified with, felt.
Often enabling feedback from other group members led to helpful insights.
Encouragement, support, friendship were all vital parts of group process. One
child's self-exposure to their vulnerability gave permission to another. I was a
container for all this, as was the group itself, which provided security within
which individuals could expose vulnerable layers of themselves which were
usually well defended. The group could be a place to test out different forms

of communication, a place to consolidate self image, a place for release of pent-up emotion, a place for emotional support.

Keeping the pictures and models provided a diary of events shared by the group. My safe-keeping of the work was another way of psychologically containing the individual and group process.

Conclusion

When I reflect on the art group I realise it forms one of the most rewarding and enjoyable parts of my working week. I was touched to hear the group sharing similar feelings when introducing two new members to the group. Although the group is often a place for grappling with difficult emotions, it is also a place for play, and a place of security and warmth. It seems that playing with art materials in an unpressurised way is nourishing, and sustains the client through the more demanding aspects of self-disclosure.

I have attempted to convey to the reader something of the potential of this kind of art therapy group. This potential never feels exhausted. The challenge is always there for me as a therapist, to make as creative use as possible of this space, balancing the needs of the individual, the group, and the wider community. The culture takes time to establish itself. This group is now oversubscribed. We have had to set limits on newcomers. Over time I hope it enhance the possibilities that individuals have of relating to their own and to others' feelings.

Chapter 7

Art Therapy with People with Learning Difficulties

Edward Kuczaj

Introduction

Recently, during a session with a client I realised that I could actually just 'be' with him, allowing him to use the space provided at his pace, without my expectations and hopes coming through. I, too, had relaxed. What was more revealing about the situation was that earlier, before the start of the session when I had collected him from his group home, he had been quite disruptive, refusing to get out of his chair and becoming quite agitated. Having allowed him there, he calmed down and finally came to the session, although still a little agitated. As the session went on and I sat back doing nothing but giving him my attention, he slowly, very slowly, started to look towards me and then towards the drawing board in front of us. A smile then came to his face and he made a gesture to indicate that he might pick up the stick of charcoal in front of him. After nearly fifteen minutes he did, drawing a line on the paper and then immediately gave the charcoal to me, for me to draw my line. The game had started.

I realised during this session the very subtle pressures at play when working with people with learning difficulties, especially those clients who have a number of additional problems alongside their initial impairment.

Working with clients with learning difficulties is not a new field for art therapists to find themselves in, but it is still a field that often requires art therapy to justify itself.

My own experience of working with this client group is spread over fifteen years. After originally training as a registered nurse for the mentally handicapped, I then worked in a number of hostels as a staff nurse and deputy charge nurse, until I left the field completely to take a degree in fine art. In full circle, I then returned to the same hospital where I had originally trained, to be employed as an art instructor, in charge of the handicraft department.

As my interest developed in the use of art, so my awareness and interest in art therapy also grew. This, with the help of a sympathetic and aware manager, led to my secondment to the Art Therapy Diploma Course (part time) at St. Albans.

Shortly after I started my course the handicraft department changed to an art therapy department. Today, it serves both hospital patients and a growing number of community clients, and currently employs two art therapists.

Like many large institutions, it is already starting to close its doors, and by 1993, it will be closed completely and replaced by group homes and hostels.

Within the institution many types of individual exist, not just those with a learning difficulty, but also those whose social circumstances forty or fifty years ago led to their admission, for reasons such as being or having an illegitimate child, or being delinquent with what was measured as a low intelligence.

The art therapist then finds him- or herself with a considerable variety of clients, with abilities and disabilities all given one title, 'learning difficulty' or what was formerly known as 'mental handicap'.

In this chapter I hope to show the role of art therapy in working with people with learning difficulties, the range of clients art therapy is able to serve and the depth of the emotional needs of those same people.

Working within a Philosophy of Care

It has to be clearly stated and understood that the term 'learning difficulties' or what was previously termed 'mental handicap' is but a blanket attempt to categorise a number of wide-ranging impairments that affect approximately three per thousand of the population. Although some of the causes can be found in genetic abnormalities, eg Down's syndrome or environmental factors such as oxygen deficiency at birth or nutritional deficiency, it is only possible to ascribe a definite cause in just under sixty per cent of cases (Heaton-Ward, 1977) Alongside this, the range of abilities, both physical and mental, vary enormously from one end of the spectrum to the other, from those who have profound learning difficulties to mild to borderline learning difficulties. Needless to say, the needs of each individual vary enormously and can impose many demands upon the art therapist, who may well attempt to serve all.

My work as an art instructor gave me a chance to view the nature of the care of people with learning difficulties in a more objective way, and made me openly question my role and aims in working with this client group. What I realised at first hand, quite abruptly, was the way the institution, (staff and residents) believed strongly in the notion of *producing*, of being able to make and/or sell objects made in a number of the occupational therapy departments.

The problem that unfortunately existed with this aim, was that there was a steadily increasing number of residents within the hospital who were incapable of reaching such a standard of competence, and who were replacing many of the higher ability residents (who were being discharged into the community) in many of the training situations.

A work or vocational philosophy originated with the establishment of the institutions themselves, when public opinion viewed the segregation of the 'mentally handicapped' as necessary in order to save society from a 'dangerous' degeneracy.

Many independent institutions organised their own farms and workshops for both productive and training work. The workshops have carried through right to this day, with contract work and other 'saleable' commodities being produced.

Alongside this philosophy, social skills training has also developed as a major concern within the care of people with learning difficulties. Linked very closely to the social skills we all need to function in our own lives, these skills have been used perhaps to bring a sense of direction to what often seems an area of work full of unknowns and uncertainties.

The importance and the narrowness of these philosophies became apparent when I attempted, as a therapist concerned with the emotional needs of individuals, to position myself within the overall philosophy of care. When I tried to do this, I realised that the emotional needs of these people have, by and large, been totally ignored until quite recently.

A belief that they showed no real emotional feelings has long been accepted within the confines of an institution. This may be due to the institution's characteristics of rigidity and conformity which leave little room for personal expression of feelings. In an article relating to the grieving process in people with learning difficulties, Lorraine Crick (1988) gives examples of the possible strengths clients have to help them through the bereavement process, although, as she points out, they are likely to be outweighed by weaknesses. These strengths are:

i) Resistance from past experiences to new changes.

ii) The rigid structure of daily activities helping to maintain normality.

iii) An ability to relate to and trust new people.

iv) An experience of dependence which helps them to accept new situations.

Perhaps the structure that clients and staff find themselves in helps perpetuate this denial of feelings, along with the staff inadequacies in ward situations which have prevailed until quite recently. The denial has a historical background, but is also linked with the prevalent assumption that a more limited cognitive capacity indicates a more limited emotional capacity.

Use of a Creative Medium

Creative media have been used for many years with people with learning difficulties, but usually in relation to the production of a set object, with the standards and restrictions that this entails. Working in an environment that took away concrete goals, that set its main goal as being non-judgemental, I soon realised the potential for the use of art.

Working with people with a mixture of abilities as an art instructor in the handicraft department, I witnessed positive changes. Although many of the clients involved initially regarded the introduction of art materials as something childish, it was only a short time before they allowed themselves the freedom to create. Taking away the rigid set of goals and definite training plans allowed a very different kind of relationship to flourish between clients and staff. Often we would work together, encouraging by example, working alongside the clients. An individual's development was always seen in relationship to that individual's own achievements, never in comparison with others.

Developmentally, the use of art as a creative medium can encourage very gently one's own self confidence and self esteem, together with physical and intellectual areas of ability. The range of clients attending the department varied considerably, including a number of individuals who presented behaviour problems, eg disturbed or aggressive outbursts. For these individuals there was, for a short time, a focus. It would be wrong and too easy to say that they channelled their aggressions in a more constructive direction, and more truthful to say that their involvement gave us, both staff and other residents, a different view of that person, seeing past the behaviour, moving from negative to positive.

A number of clients pointed to a need for a more structured and more intimate relationship. Repetition of images, together with specific expressions of anger and unease in relation to specific images, made me appreciate the need for a different approach and a greater openness on my (and the institution's) part to their emotions.

Art Therapy

The use of art as a creative medium is generally understood as relevant to the field of learning difficulties, in providing a useful component part of their growth. Art therapy aims to be more specific in terms of its role when dealing with someone's emotional state or behaviour. In doing this it sets itself firmly to one side from the sometimes very general nature of 'art' itself, namely the production of an object and the opportunity for judgements relating to that object. Art therapy with this client group necessitates a clear aim and role, especially because the field of learning difficulties, as stated before, covers a wide spectrum. We cannot presume that all clients and residents require developmental work, social training, or art therapy, just because they are included under this heading. Is there a magic point at which art therapy becomes appropriate within this wide spectrum?

Within the development of my own work I have seen a gradual shift in emphasis within the client groupings. It was easy at first, as no doubt other therapists have found, to open the doors to almost whatever referral came my way. It was a time to test the theory and the practice, and this was important for me, and for professionals around me.

Areas of Work

All art therapists are fortunately unique individuals, bringing to their work their own concerns, characteristics, personalities and potential. This therefore, to some extent, dictates the emphasis they will place on their own areas of work and involvement. I would like now to discuss the areas of work I am involved in and which I feel are appropriate for art therapy involvement. This is a response to the needs I see around me, and the result of my attempts to prioritise the service the art therapy department is attempting to provide.

The main areas of work the department is involved in, both within the hospital and the community, are listed below and I will later explain them with specific examples.

       i) relationship development
      ii) emotional disturbance
     iii) challenging behaviour

iv) resettlement work in groups.

Although 'relationships' is placed here separately from emotional disturbance and challenging behaviour, very often it is a problem present within these other areas and vice versa.

Looking now at some specific cases, I would like to explore these areas and illustrate some of the issues involved, when working with art therapy and people with learning difficulties.

Relationship Development

When working with clients, one issue clearly underlined is the lack of any kind of basic relationship with another individual in all but a few cases. This is even more acute with the higher-dependency clients or those who experience consistent behaviour problems. Relationships that do develop in these cases can very often be negative ones. The problem is often a lack of point of contact when faced with someone who presents so many needs, and our own feelings of loss or failure can creep in when attempting to care for this person.

Carol had attended the art department prior to the conversion to an art therapy department. In her mid-thirties, she had lived most of her life in a high-dependency ward. Although seemingly quite intellectually impaired, she had a number of self-help skills and presented herself as quite an independent character. Although there were no verbal communication skills, she understood most requests or suggestions with the help of gestural prompts. She was still very isolated, not forming any close relationships, and quite obsessional and ritualistic in her behaviour.

Her attendance at open art sessions prior to any therapeutic involvement was always quite extraordinary. She would spend most of the session collecting various coloured objects from around her and then placing them in strict sequences in front of her. Very often she would peep from the corner of her eye, checking to see who was looking before making a mad dash to a cupboard to fetch more material or objects. Crayons, pens, sometimes taken from other residents, would be placed in front of her on the table.

Obsessional behaviour is very common in people with learning difficulties. Rocking, finger play, stepping on various parts of a floor are not uncommon in a number of residents, perhaps a sign of deprivation of stimulating experiences throughout their lives, leading to a reliance upon themselves for stimulation. For Carol it seemed that the self-stimulation had this role, but to make it more personalised she would, at each arrangement, touch each object with her finger which would have a small drop of saliva on it. On paper small strokes of each colour crayon would be placed, again each with a dab of saliva. Her need and persistence to do this was quite extreme, and she would become quite agitated if unable to do so. Marks were observed on her legs in set patterns where she had picked the skin, and she would often mark her clothes with various colours in strict patterns.

Working with a therapist in an individual session once a week for one hour, she was allowed to continue the use of her 'collage', but encouraged to interact with the therapist. Attempts had been made before to engage her interest, encouraging her to colour in squared paper. This proved to be too rigid and only showed a compliance on her part with someone else's requests, giving them her attention for the minimum amount of time. By allowing Carol to relax within the session and encouraging her then by the gentle use of 'reflective drawing', she allowed herself, trusting the situation, to interact. The 'reflective drawing' took the form of handing the crayon or pen backwards and forwards, shifting the point of responsibility between the therapist and client. The images made by the therapist were at first very simple, but it soon became apparent that Carol understood the nature of the 'game' and was willing to participate. Drawing a simple figure, Carol copied and the result can be seen in *Figure 7.1*.

Figure 7.1 - Reflective image

It was difficult to judge whether she had any true recognition that the drawing was of a figure, but what was more important was the very definite tolerance she was showing in letting someone be with her for an increasing amount of time at each session. This was confirmed later when one day, after walking into the department, she went up to the therapist who had been working with her, and gave her a hug. From an individual who had always been seen to be reclusive and unapproachable, it seemed a very positive statement.

For many individuals, the framework that art therapy provides gives the opportunity for that individual to develop and experience a relationship other than one of a receiver accepting all the time from a provider.

A great many of the clients who are seen under the heading of 'relationship development' are those clients of high dependency, who usually have few or no communication skills. With this group there is a need for a gentle approach where expectations remain low.

Art therapy is, whether as a primary or secondary concern, about a visual experience and contact with it, but this is often placed to one side with the clients in this field of work. What then becomes important is the space provided, the time, attention and continuity.

Sessions with clients whose impairment is such that verbal dialogue and understanding is limited, and who remain isolated and withdrawn, require firstly the making of a 'space'. The space becomes a situation where expectations remain low and discreet, where just 'being' with another person is the main concern. Very often sessions revolve around times as small as a few minutes, long before an hour can be contemplated. It is at these times that one begins to take stock of the possible impoverishments in social contacts, which due to lack of early bonding and sensory stimulation, have probably never existed to any length or depth in their life.

Often the therapist can act as facilitator for other inputs once initial problems relating to length and depth of interaction have been resolved. This gives rise to an interesting question that we should ask, as a therapy offering a specific type of relationship to cover very basic needs for people with learning difficulties. Are we the best providers, and should we be the sole providers, when our input is so often limited and restricted? As the conditions of care gradually improve, and more time becomes available for individual attention from other care staff, this question will need to be looked at more seriously.

Emotional Disturbance

A large proportion of the work carried out within the art therapy service, both within the hospital and within the community, is with clients who present emotionally disturbed behaviour. The behaviour is often directed inwards in physical terms, eg as obsessional behaviour, introversion or self injury.

Mental illness is sadly not well acknowledged within the field of learning difficulties, and dysfunctional behaviours are often associated with the original condition, instead of with changing life circumstances or environment. Surveys of mental illness in people with learning difficulties living within institutions show an incidence of about eight to ten per cent (Heaton-Ward, 1977). They are liable, as we are, to the full range of mental illnesses.

Bereavement, and more especially general loss relating to various life changes and movements, has been a completely neglected area, one that is only now being acknowledged.

An institution or caring situation can disguise many problems. The structure of daily activities, supervision of normal living and the sheer number of changes (staff and resident moves) that can occur within a client's life, may override (for some) many of the initial feelings relating to a loss or change. A client, Laura, was referred because of poor self esteem, low confidence, general lack of interest in herself (physical care) and an underlying anger. In her early twenties, she still maintained a close relationship with her family, from whom she had been parted in her early teens. Her learning difficulty was mild, and she attended a local training centre. One major problem was her frequent incontinence (seemingly deliberate) that occurred prior to her getting out of bed in the morning. She was due to be resettled back to her own health authority outside Bristol in a small group home, which would be nearer her parents.

Introducing clients into sessions is often difficult because of their own expectations of art. As with other client groups, fear of lack of ability is often an issue to be worked through. By drawing with clients, at their level, and introducing oneself, the problems can be addressed. Laura was seen once a week for one hour, as were the majority of clients. Themes were given initially but it was found that she was more than willing to share experiences. All the time she spoke of home, describing her mother and father in glowing terms, and it became clear that she wanted to live at home with them rather than live in a small group home. *Figure 7.2* shows a plan of Laura's home, her bedroom situated on the right at the top of the stairs, with the bathroom separating her own room from her parents. During a break in the sessions, Laura's grandmother died and at the following session she painted quite freely the grave with its flowers. She acknowledged the image but said she preferred not to talk about it. It was only at the next session that she could relate how she felt about her grandmother and talk about the day of the funeral. Laura had on that day stayed with a neighbour to 'look after' her nephew, visiting the grave the next day.

Figure 7.2 - Plan of Laura's home

Bereavement places many burdens on individuals and, unfortunately, having a 'handicapped' child becomes an extra burden at the time of a death. It is common for individuals not to attend their own family's funerals, sometimes not even visiting the grave, so Laura was therefore more fortunate than some. In subsequent sessions she drew her Gran's favourite fish that she liked to eat, and an outing she had been on many years earlier with both grandparents, indicating perhaps her growing acceptance of the death.

She still spoke warmly about home and asked one day to make a wooden model of a table for her eldest brother who was a carpenter. Laura was the second child of her mother's first marriage, her father having died when she was four. Her mother had then remarried with subsequent brothers and sisters following. During a session when she was painting the model table, she said quite suddenly, 'If Dad found out about this, he would be furious and jealous.' After encouragement to go on at her own pace, she explained that her real father had died, and she remembered and related what had happened. In a mixture of

past and present tense she spoke of her real father and a dislike for her
stepfather, who said 'horrible things to her'. The 'horrible things' were her
stepfather's attempts to control her incontinence with a threat not to have her
home at weekends. There were also times at home when she felt Stepdad came
between herself and her mother.

Overall, after talking to the ward team, it seemed that Laura's father was
being quite realistic about the situation, and knew that Laura would not be
coming back home to live. Her mother accepted this as well, but apparently
whilst acknowledging the need to talk about this issue to Laura, found it a
difficult problem to face.

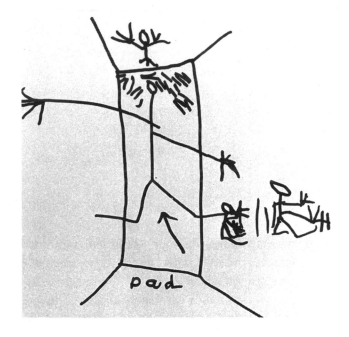

Figure 7.3 - 'Funny' Event

Laura's understanding and insight into her feelings are further highlighted in
figure 7.3. Here she had drawn a 'funny' event in the past. Stepfather is asleep
on a sun lounger and her brother comes from behind and pours a bucket of
water over him. On the right hand side of the picture she then drew Dad chasing
her brother. As she explained the picture she laughed. When asked if she would
like to be the one throwing the water, she laughed again and agreed.

At the end of six months Laura was resettled into a small group home near her parents. The move was presented as being permanent and her parents were encouraged to endorse this fact. Sessions at this point related to the move and seemed positive, with images of the house and possible future pets she could have. Laura moved quite happily, but whether her feelings have only been temporarily subdued remains to be seen, as no continuation of therapy was possible.

Whilst Laura's behaviour was 'inward', often clients can be more direct in approach. Jill, a client from the community, was referred because of her difficulties in maintaining relationships with individuals around her, and her general exclusion from activities within the training centre she attended, because of her disruptive behaviour. Whilst she might be noisy, occasionally pushing over a chair, she would never be physically angry with anyone.

Her difficulty in maintaining relationships arose from her obsessions with specific individuals, an almost 'teenager crush' to the point where the individual could accept no more. She would follow the person around, waiting sometimes outside their house to see them during the evening. When they then became upset and intolerant of the situation, Jill would then become upset too. Jill was in her mid-twenties and would always choose a female (usually older) for the relationship, including sometimes a member of staff. Her learning difficulty was relatively mild and she was very independent in most ways, living at home with her mother and brother. Her father was separated from her mother and had left home a number of years ago, maintaining no apparent contact

With clients who have the capacity of understanding, a form of contract between the therapist and client is always given. In Jill's case, boundaries of the session (times, regularity) and also what was allowed and not allowed (ie physical injury to the therapist) were given. The boundaries were tested many times at first, with her appearance at the sessions after twenty minutes or so. Often this lateness revolved around difficulties she was experiencing with 'friends' within the training centre where the sessions took place.

Anger towards people round her sometimes spilled over into the session. On one occasion she was encouraged to take her anger out and express it on paper. She scribbled for a minute or so, and then pushed the chairs over and started to cry. After ten minutes of her crying, we could then start to talk about her feelings. At the end of the session she picked up the various bits and pieces and said that she felt better about the situation that had caused her feelings. The anger had been contained within the room, but more importantly she had been allowed to become angry, experiencing with someone else this part of herself in a constructive way.

The majority of the sessions revolved around images of herself and someone who was her 'friend' at that moment. There was little talk of home and her obsession persisted around developing a female relationship. At one session, while talking about what made a good friend, a theme was suggested of a happy event in the past with someone she knew and liked a good deal. *Figure 7.4* is the result, and shows the day her grandmother died, a far from happy event which had occurred four or five years previously. Jill and Mum are placed on the left, with Gran and her brother on the right. Everyone except Gran is drawn in black, Gran being drawn in pink. Also in the image is an ambulance and a hearse. There were no tears, only regrets that Gran was no longer alive, and feelings that Jill missed her. At a later session looking at the same image, her feeling became more expressive and tears were shed. It appeared that her desire for establishing a 'deep' relationship with a female might stem from her relationship with her grandmother, with whom she had been very close, combined with the lack of relationship with her father.

Figure 7.4 - A Happy Event

Over a period of nearly a year of regular sessions she became, within those sessions, quite comfortable, and she was able to express her feelings more openly, including her frustrations. Although her basic needs have not changed as such, progress has been made at perhaps looking more directly at the problem. It is hoped that it may be possible within the near future to include her in a group where her attitudes to males as well as females can be explored. Art therapy for Jill has become a regular channel for her feelings.

Challenging Behaviour

The term 'challenging behaviour' is now a common term used with a specific group of people with learning difficulties who experience major problems. It has many connotations and is often hard to define. A useful and concise definition may be found in the Kings Fund Document(1987), which gives a clear statement of challenging behaviour:

> 'Severely challenging behaviour refers to behaviour of such an intensity, frequency or duration that the physical safety of the person, or others, is likely to be placed in serious jeopardy or behaviour which is likely to seriously limit or delay access to and use of ordinary community facilities.'

The term is widely used and often covers a multitude of sins. However, for the service that the department offers, it represents an increasingly important and major part of our work. The causes are many, and lie largely within major emotional disturbances and forms of mental illness. Treatment has remained largely behavioural in approach, together with drug therapy. In such a traditional area of treatment, the introduction of a psychotherapeutic medium alongside this approach has had to be a slow and careful one.

What has become very apparent are the different criteria that people can place on clients who exhibit challenging behaviour. With the move to the community, levels of 'acceptability' have been raised as many clients find themselves in a very different kind of environment. The very clear boundaries that therapy offers fit in well with the needs of these clients, providing a structure in a seemingly difficult and problematic area.

Work on a disturbed male ward has led to a positive input with clients. Those referred with persistent behavioural problems are seen in a small room on the ward. As well as offering a secure environment for the therapist, this also helps to limit the potential for opting out of sessions.

One particular client, John, who suffered from paranoia superimposed upon a mild learning difficulty, would initially continually come up with ways of avoiding sessions: 'I'm too busy, I can't see you tomorrow' or he might, on arrival on the ward, be complaining of feeling ill, saying he was going to lie on his bed. Every time, when he was told that I would be in the room anyway for the hour, whether he came or not, he would come, forgetting about his previous excuses. John's initial desire for avoidance would often bring about visits and meetings outside the sessions with requests for postponement or cancellation of the next session.

The amount of insight and understanding clients have in relation to themselves and their images is as variable as the range of learning difficulties. There is of course the danger of reading too much into too little, of attributing emotional and psychological reasonings to behaviour in order to 'fill the gap'. However, there is the equal and more prevalent danger of attributing behaviours to a client's original learning difficulties to 'fill the gap' even more efficiently, in our desire for understanding.

Many of the behaviours that are treated as 'challenging' can be seen in terms of self-preservation, of building a boundary for protection from others. Clients who are resistant to change will often use their behaviour to sabotage an input from a therapist, in the hope of returning to their original position. The continuity that a therapist can provide within a set framework challenges this. Very rarely does this mean that the therapist will then be subjected to repeated aggressive attacks. The 'weapon' given to the client is their ability and ultimate decision to leave the session if they wish, at any time. John, after a few months questioned me why I always stayed the hour, and asked what he would have to do to make me go early. When I questioned why this was important to him, he proceeded to say 'On yer bike, on yer bike.' This went on for a few minutes or so, only to be repeated later. Smiling all the time, he finally said 'You're not going to go, are you?' Needless to say, clients can he even more direct in their desire to opt out of sessions, eg by displaying disturbed or aggressive behaviour. However, because of the low expectations that the therapist places on the client, direct confrontations are not everyday occurrences.

One of the greatest benefits of a therapist working with a person on challenging behaviour is the positive attitude he or she can bring to the problem. There is often a 'knock-on' effect to other staff/team members when they can see concrete results, as in images, occurring during the sessions. It can also, in some cases, bring into question the assumptions made by professionals about the awareness and understanding that clients may or may not have.

Another client referred for challenging behaviour was Martin, labelled in the past as schizophrenic. He had a severely deprived background and used self-mutilation as a form of stimulation and means of obtaining attention. He

Figure 7.5 - Martin's drawing

Figure 7.6 - Therapist and Client

had over the years manoeuvered himself into a position where he could dictate what happened, by his willingness (or lack of it) to participate in various activities.

Although his verbal communication was limited, revolving around mono-syllables which were at times quite hard to discern, his symmetrical images suggest a more detailed side to his character. Houses featured in many of his pictures, such as *figure 7.5*, and when questioned, he would repeat the name of a hostel he once lived in with his brother. Sessions at first lasted a matter of minutes, the number of images produced often ruled by the number of clean sheets of paper! Many were simple repetitive patterns, and interaction during the session could only be broadened very slowly. It was difficult to judge the importance of the sessions for him, but the image in *figure 7.6* gave a new insight. Without any prompt or theme, he chose to draw the session itself, therapist and client together! The clarity and detail within the image is quite astounding, and revealed a much more complex, and deeper side to Martin, especially in terms of his awareness of his surroundings and the events he was involved in. With Martin, the continuity and tolerance are important, enabling sessions to gradually increase to forty minutes.

In all the areas in which the department works, challenging behaviour has become the most involving and demanding in terms of referrals, both from within the hospital and from the community. This reflects not only the depart-ment's interest, but more importantly the qualities that art therapy has to offer these needs.

Resettlement Work in Groups

The hospital's impending closure highlighted the need for a clear resettlement programme that gave attention to all aspects of care of an individual from social skills through to emotional needs. Looking primarily at these emotional needs, the department decided to offer (and is offering) art therapy for groups of residents moving out to small group homes.

The main aim of the resettlement work is to provide a forum for a group of clients (normally between four and six) to look at difficulties/problems that might arise with a move, looking especially at their own expectations and hopes related to the move.

Although usually offered for a set period covering the time before and after the move has taken place, it can in some instances last significantly longer, in one case a year, when a move was continually put back.

The sessions are used as a time to focus upon the basics of the move, ie 'which room is mine and what colour will it be?' as well as looking at group interaction and encouraging individual development. The sessions also high-light individual relationships within the group and behaviour towards each other. Although staff are usually involved, their attendance can be inconsistent because of staffing pressures and other commitments. These groups usually find that the use of visual images, which can be looked at again and again, keeps the move in a positive light. When delays occur, causing clients and staff to doubt whether the move will ever happen, these past images can be used to re-focus the group, often lifting spirits in the process.

Group work in other areas is often harder to initiate and is proving a more difficult part of the department's work to establish, simply because of the very diverse range of abilities of clients. In this respect grouping on a relatively similar level becomes difficult.

Conclusion

Art therapy is not a panacea for all difficulties, and as a relatively new therapy in this field, it is sometimes seen as a last resort after trying everything else. However, it does have specific qualities very appropriate for these clients, eg

  1) creative involvement
  2) non-judgemental nature
  3) potential for expression of self at their own pace
  4) a time and place
  5) an image that can be kept

This last point is very important for a large number of individuals, who have little opportunity to keep personal belongings in complete security.

Although the work is not seen as 'developmental', many clients do, through their therapy sessions, develop new skills and awareness. In this way a kind of informal teaching, usually client-led, takes place. Social skills may also fall within the session, but these, whilst not denying their place and role, are seen as by-products of the session, something a little extra. What has become apparent to me, within my work, is the specific role art therapy can play for people with learning difficulties. Art therapy is a diverse therapy and the therapists within it sometimes have diverse roles, but, to be seen as a therapy in its own right, it needs to portray a relatively clear image. In our field of work, this has led to a concentration in the main areas of emotional disturbance and challenging behaviour. Referrals to art therapists are often couched in terms of 'he likes art', giving rise to a feeling that referrers are probably unsure about what art therapy is. A clear identity, with a tremendous amount of groundwork, pays many dividends, including better informed referrers.

Specifically for people with learning difficulties, art therapy gives the therapist a possibility of working with a client (and the client responding) in a relaxed way. Much of the work with these individuals, by the various professions involved with them, is far from relaxed, the thought being that progress has to be made. What happens very often is that the client, the real client, is then missed. Working with people with learning difficulties very often gives rise to a feeling of working in the dark. Timescales that have so much meaning in our everyday life often become meaningless, and changes we may wish to see in our clients are often slow to come. Changes can occur, but always at the client's own speed.

Attitudes and approaches to this field of work have moved greatly over the years, to the point where we now speak of 'people with learning difficulties'. However, we are unfortunately still left with a label that tries to explain neatly a vast array of individual problems. Although there are similarities, the problems are very varied in kind and in degree of severity. There is a tremendous need for a 'holistic' approach relating to the care of people with learning difficulties, and art therapists along with the other professions have a specific and positive role to play.

Chapter 8

'It Just Happened'

Looking at Crime Events

Marian Liebmann

Introduction

The purpose of this chapter is to look mainly at one particular way of using art with offenders, in the context of a local probation office. First I explain this context and the way offenders come to be on probation. Then I outline how I came to use art to look at offending behaviour, and then use some examples to show how this works in practice, with individuals and with groups. Finally, I include a few pointers concerning the way this method can lead on to further work using art therapy.

Offenders and the Probation Context

It is important to remember that offenders do not always conform to the public image portrayed in the media, but include a normal range of human beings - men, women, young people, adults (occasionally elderly but rarely), extroverts, introverts, cheerful and helpful, angry and destructive. Offenders commit crimes for a wide variety of reasons, and it is not always obvious what these are. Many relevant sociological texts have been written on this subject, but in this chapter I am only able to consider those personal reasons over which an offender might have some control.

The British criminal justice system has many ways of dealing with offenders. Imprisonment has always been central to the system, although there is increasing dissatisfaction with it. It is expensive, and experience has shown that, although it contains offenders for a period, it can do little to reform or

rehabilitate them. Fines are usually used for small offences, where the offender
can pay. There are also newer disposals such as an Attendance Centre Order
(a mixture of physical education, craft and discussion groups, held on Satur-
days), and a Community Service Order (unpaid work for the local community).
Prison sentences can now be suspended in part or whole, so that offenders have
a 'last chance', and only go to prison if they re-offend. For very minor offences,
a court may grant a Conditional Discharge, where no more will be said unless
the person re-offends.

Probation orders are used for clients who need counselling or help with
social problems, especially where these problems have an obvious connection
with their offence, eg alcoholism, marriage breakdown, family problems,
poverty. Probation officers work with clients both on their offending behaviour
and on the causes that lie behind them. They are trained social workers and can
work with clients in many different ways according to need. Clients remain in
the community, and come to the probation office or receive visits at home, for
a specified period (the shortest probation order is six months, the longest three
years).

Another aspect of the work of the probation service is the provision of
'social Inquiry Reports' to courts, to help them arrive at a realistic sentence,
taking account of the offender's personal and family circumstances. It is often
at this stage that discussion starts concerning the reasons why someone has
offended, and what needs to be done to put things right.

By law, a client has to agree to a probation order being made, but given that
the alternative may be worse, many clients' commitment may only be skin-
deep! For these, probation becomes a form of control in that all clients have to
be seen regularly.

However, many clients do genuinely want to solve their problems, and they
negotiate individual contracts with their probation officers. For instance, clients
may opt to work on practical problems such as budgeting, job search, accommodation, to improve their circumstances and remove the need to break the
law. Some attend specialised groups, eg alcohol, anger control, driving education, women's group, sex offenders' group etc, where they learn from films,
exercises and discussions about the effects of their offence, and methods of
staying out of trouble. Others benefit from individual counselling or from
taking a look at their attitudes and ways of thinking. Often the actual offence
is the tip of the iceberg, and brings to light problems that have been left
unattended for years. For all clients who are trying to make some change in
their lives, however small, probation can be a challenging experience.

The probation service has a wide range of facilities, which can vary from area to area. There are hostels and day centres, as well as the groups already described. Clients can attend some of these voluntarily, and others by order of the courts. Many probation officers have special interests or qualifications in such diverse matters as community work, psychotherapy or mountain leadership, and this provides further resources for probation clients.

Most probation day centres run a programme of activities, and art is often among the choices available. These sessions may be run like an art class with tuition available, or as a means of helping clients develop a recreational activity. In these cases an art teacher or instructor is usually employed. However, in some day centres, there is a recognition of the potential for art as a means of personal communication or as an integral part of clients' self-development, and in this case art therapists may be employed.

Art therapy can then be available to clients on the same basis as for any other client group. Again there are many ways of doing this. Clients may all be working on their own projects, and engage in individual discussion of these with the art therapist. Or they may work in a group, using a common theme, sometimes related to problems shared by the group. In such a group, the period of activity is usually followed by a period in which group members share their work, and further discussion often develops from this.

As well as the general use of art therapy with some probation clients, there is one technique I find particularly useful with almost all clients, especially at the start of a probation order. The next section describes this.

Looking at Crime Events

All probation clients, by definition, have committed an offence, and found themselves in court. For many, this is a traumatic event, and they do not always understand what led up to it. For them it is often something that 'just happened'. Even some of the 'old-timers' who have many criminal convictions and who are well used to appearing in court, may remain unsure exactly how the same cycle of events keeps repeating itself, seeing their crimes as 'unfortunate circumstances' over which they have little or no control.

The use of a narrative technique, by drawing 'comic strip' stories, can help clients describe the crime event, as seen from their point of view. This can help them become more aware of the events leading up to the crime, and then to see where they could devise alternatives with less disastrous consequences. This process can also help to pin-point patterns in offences which may not be obvious from talking about them, and suggest areas for future work.

One advantage of using 'comic strips' is that clients are involved, and can often contribute more fully than by using words, especially as many clients have poor verbal skills. Most probation clients are already familiar with comic strips as a means of communication and this helps them to get started. The results are then available for shared discussion, and the process can be inspected.

This idea developed out of previous work with offenders in a day centre where I discovered that many of them enjoyed using art and seemed more at ease communicating in this way than with words. When more recently I joined a probation field team, I decided to try and see if I could use art in this more individual context. There seemed no reason against using drawing rather than talking as a counselling method.

I started by asking one of my first clients if he would be prepared to use art, and he agreed. I suggested a comic strip format as it was likely to be familiar to him, and therefore not too threatening. In the event the process threw up more information than I would have gleaned verbally over several months, so I was encouraged to continue. As I began to use comic strips with other clients, I found the format particularly useful in opening up discussion of the crime events that had originally led to court and probation.

When offenders are placed on probation, the first few sessions (usually weekly) are used for assessment. There is already a fair idea of the problem areas from the report-writing stage, but this needs to be translated into a plan for action, eg to prioritise the areas to work on first. As the offence is what has brought someone to probation, that will usually be one of the most important topics to discuss.

It is at this stage that I usually mention the possibility of using art. If I know the client is interested in art (eg from discussion at the 'Social Inquiry Report' stage), I usually tell them I am too, and suggest we can use pictures to look at some of the areas of work, especially their offences.

If there is no such indication, I might introduce the idea of a 'comic strip' as a way of telling me more about the offence and how the client sees it. Some clients refuse (usually out of embarrassment at their drawing ability) and I do not press them. There are also some offences which do not lend themselves to this method, such as those that have taken place on a continuous basis.

When a client starts on a comic strip, he or she often needs prompting, either out of embarrassment, or because it is difficult to remember, or is a jumbled incomprehensible event that 'just happened'. The drawing of the cartoon strip becomes a dialogue between me and the client to draw out as much information and as many stages as possible. I always try to keep close to the client's experience and the way he or she sees and experiences what has happened.

When a client has (to the best of his or her ability) completed a comic strip for a particular offence, we look at it together, side by side. This provides an opportunity for clients to distance themselves from what happened, and to see events in their lives as if for the first time. They may also begin to see themselves as actors at the centre of the story rather than as victims of circumstances. This is an essential step on the road to becoming responsible people who have some control over their actions and their future.

The following examples illustrate how I used this method in practice with individuals.

Examples in Practice: Individuals

Often the 'first go' at a comic strip only tells half the story. The first example shows how the process showed up gaps that were later filled in.

Don: a problem of violence

Don was a sixteen year old who had assaulted a girl. He was very ashamed of his offence and hoped never to do such a thing again. However, his former school told me of his violence there, and his mother related how he was following in his father's footsteps - she had divorced Don's father for serious and continuing violence against her and the two children. Don had been to a special school, and could hardly read or write at all, but had enjoyed art, so was quite happy to go along with my suggestion of using pictures.

I started by asking Don to do a comic strip of the offence. His first attempt (*figure 8.1*) was only four 'frames' long. It shows Don meeting up with his friend who tells him a girl they know is being bullied, and Don agrees to take the day off work to 'sort it out'. They wait all day by the school and then the children start to come out. The final frame shows Don hitting the girl who is supposed to be the bully.

Most of the vital links still seemed to be missing, so the next week I asked him to go a bit more slowly and put in more detail after the third frame and before he actually hit the girl. I hoped that, by slowing down the process using drawing, I might help Don to be more aware of the external and internal factors which led to the disastrous conclusion, and thereby have some hope of eventually controlling the process. *Figure 8.2* shows the next version.

The first frame shows the alleged bully being pointed out. Then Don goes up to her and accosts her; in frame 3 he hits her and in frame 4 finishes it off

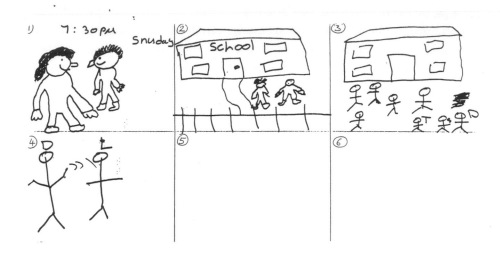

Figure 8.1 - Don's offence: first version

Figure 8.2 - Don's offence: second version

with a kick, walking away smiling in frame 5. It is only as he goes home with the girl who 'hired' him that he begins to feel panicky and starts to run. He told me that he had only meant to tell the bully off, but when she told him to mind his own business and used the words 'Fuck off, you great big fat bastard', he lost control and hit her. I got him to tell me the details of the conversation and took it down verbatim.

We used these pictures to look at the starting point where Don was asked to do someone else's dirty work, and he began to see that he was being used. He realised that the same had happened at school, where he was often the 'sorter-out' and was in repeated trouble. He knew his teachers had become very exasperated with him because he always appeared to be sorry, but then repeated his behaviour next time. He said he sometimes felt he had a good person and a bad person inside himself and was never quite sure when the one would turn into the other. I asked him to draw me pictures of the 'Good Don' and the 'Bad Don', and he seemed to enjoy these.

The next week we explored these images, and how they differed. The 'Good Don' could talk about things, come to arrangements with people and wouldn't go into the situation in the first place. The 'Bad Don' liked fights and just got involved in them. We looked again at the comic strip and tried to see if there were any points at which Don could have avoided hitting the girl. We listed the 'triggers' for Don and then put these on a 'feelings thermometer'. There were two sets of triggers that seemed particularly important - the first being called names like 'fatty' or 'bastard' and the second anyone hurting or insulting someone close to him, especially a friend, his brother or his mother. From this we went on to explore feelings about Don's family in general, including his father.

In the above sequence, the initial comic strip and its next version showed up immediate further points for exploration, based on Don's view of the experience. It became clear that as well as tackling his temper problem, we needed to look at his own role as 'sorter-out'. The next example shows a similar role emerging, in a different context, for a different kind of offence.

Mack: theft and loneliness

Mack was a slightly handicapped young man who spoke very slowly. He had been involved in two serious car accidents at the ages of seven and 17, and this had left him with probable slight brain damage. He had some difficulty controlling a pen. Now aged 24, he lived at home with his mother, and had a part-time job on a government scheme. He was on probation for theft of petrol.

Although the pictures Mack produced were scarcely comprehensible, the process helped him to look at the sequence of events. The comic strip showed Mack and a friend going to his brother's flat, then helping the friend fetch petrol for his motorbike. The friend cut the wire to gain access to a yard with vehicles, and persuaded Mack to climb through and siphon out some petrol. The police arrived, the friend vanished and Mack was arrested.

We then looked at what Mack could have done instead. He came up with several suggestions:

(a) Go back to his brother's flat rather than break into the yard.

(b) Stay the night at his brother's flat if no petrol.

(c) Not mind being called 'chicken'.

(d) Say 'Don't be stupid' to his friend.

(e) Say 'Do your own dirty work' to his friend.

In further discussion Mack acknowledged that others 'sweet-talked' him into trouble, and that he was meeting the wrong kind of people. He was lonely and got depressed when not working, thinking nobody wanted him, an easy prey for others more streetwise than he was, especially if they had some 'dirty work' to be done. He pinpointed his main problem as making the right sort of friends.

Shortly after this, to his mother's consternation, Mack decided to leave home and went to live with some friends. Apart from a nasty incident when he was 'framed' by some 'friends' for a crime they committed (Mack was acquitted) Mack did not reappear in court. At the end of his probation order, I asked him what he had gained from it, and he said slowly 'I tells them to do their own dirty work. I got more confidence now. I got my own friends too'.

Raymond: a family man and sex offender

Raymond was a sex offender aged 40 who had been given a two year probation order for putting his hand on a 12 year old girl's leg between the knee and crotch, while on a bus. He had committed a similar offence three years previously and had completed a two year probation order without re-offending. He was happily married with two young children, aged five and one. This was Ray's second marriage, his first (childless) having finished as a result of his previous sex offences and spells in prison. When I met him, Ray was also attending periodic appointments with the psychiatrist, who felt that his offence was a 'cry for help' due to mounting family debts. Although Ray was in full-time work, he was poorly paid, so the first priority was to start dealing with debts. Here I was fortunate to be able to link the family with an experienced debt counsellor. However, it seemed to me that Ray's particular style of 'cry for help' was unusual to say the least, and that he needed to find another way of asking for help than committing sex offences. I asked if he was willing to do some pictures about his offences, and he agreed.

I asked him to draw the sequence of events leading up to his last offence (*figure 8.3*).

Figure 8.3 - Ray's new offence

Frame 1: Early one morning, it is raining, Ray's car will not start.

Frame 2: He sets off walking to the bus for work (the nearest stop is 1.5 miles away), clutching his bag of sandwiches.

Frame 3: He just misses a bus (wheels disappearing) and waits in the rain for the next one.

Frame 4: A bus comes and Ray gets on. It is empty except for one girl.

Frame 5: Ray sits next to the girl.

Frame 6: Ray tries to get into conversation with the girl.

Frame 7: Ray puts his hand on the girl's leg. Both faces are shown looking straight ahead rather than at each other.

I had imagined that Ray had found himself squeezed into a crowded bus on a rainy day and by chance found himself next to a girl, so this strip cartoon was a complete surprise. It showed that he had chosen to sit next to the girl on an otherwise empty bus, and in discussion he admitted that the offence had been inevitable from the moment he got on the bus. We went through the sequence, trying to see where he could have acted otherwise - for example, phone into work and lose half a day's pay, sit elsewhere on the bus, get off before things got out of control, find someone to talk to about problems. Ray said he had been very depressed that morning, with thoughts going round and round his head about family debts.

Generally he saw the offence as the way he knew of finishing himself off most effectively. I asked him what he thought the girl felt, but he looked totally blank, as if he was so immersed in his own thoughts and needs that he was quite unaware of her as a person.

As all this work was based on the most recent offence, it seemed a good idea to look at the one before to see if it followed the same pattern. Ray drew this sequence out (*figure 8.4*).

Figure 8.4 - Ray's previous offence

Frame 1: Ray fills his car with petrol at a petrol station.

Frame 2: Ray speeds along the road, against a background of houses.

Frame 3: He stops at a bus stop, where a woman neighbour with a 'bit of a reputation' is waiting on her own. He offers her a lift.

Frame 4: Ray and the neighbour get into his car.

Frame 5: The car speeds away from the bus stop.

Frame 6: Ray puts his arm across onto the woman's leg. The scene is drawn from the front.

It shows a very similar pattern to the other offence. Ray chose a woman he hardly knew, who was on her own. He did not look at her while committing the offence (fortunately for other road users!) and seemed unaware of her as a person. He admitted this time that the offence had given him a 'buzz' and tried to justify it. He likened it to 'forbidden fruit', all the more attractive because of its forbiddenness, and felt he was reacting as a toddler might to parental prohibitions. Again, he found it hard to think how he might have acted differently, but finally suggested talking to someone about his worries, staying at home, or driving straight past women in lonely situations.

After our discussion concerning Ray's offences, it became clear that he had a perennial problem with fantasies of forbidden sex, and that his offences were the tip of the iceberg. He clearly needed further support and opportunities for discussion, and willingly joined a voluntary-attendance sex-offenders group, meeting fortnightly to discuss these matters. His wife supported him in this, and he became a stalwart member of the group.

There are occasions when clients agree very readily to do a comic strip, but then somehow cannot produce it. The following is one of these.

Darren: burglary and alcohol

Darren was a young man of 18 who showed considerable promise. He was tall and well built, had done reasonably well at school, and was a good amateur boxer. He had a job as a carpenter and lived at home with caring parents. He had been given a one year probation order for burglary and had also committed offences of violence. I took over his case halfway through the order.

Unfortunately, Darren seemed unwilling to talk about himself or his offences. He was late for appointments and always had something else 'important' to do, so that he stayed a minimum length of time. Meanwhile, he continued to offend, usually acts of violence to another person or criminal damage, but made light of it. I wondered if an alcohol problem might lie behind his behaviour, but he denied it.

Discovering that he had done a CSE in Art at school, I asked him to draw out a comic strip sequence for any one of his offences. For weeks he 'did not get round to it' or 'forgot it', then, just before another court appearance, he brought in his drawing (*figure 8.5*).

Figure 8.5 - Darren's burglary

The sequence shows Darren and two friends getting drunk (frame 1), and then deciding to break into a warehouse (frame 2). They found a panel at the side of the warehouse, so they broke in (frame 3). In frame 4 they carry out the 'loot'

(TVs, computers and tools), and in frame 5 they are caught in the act by the police. The final frame shows them in the cells.

When I asked Darren at what stage he could have acted differently, he pointed straight to frame 1 and said 'not get drunk'. He later added 'not hang round with mates'. Further conversation brought out the statement 'it's the drink', the first time he acknowledged that he had an alcohol problem.

It also intrigued me that Darren managed to claim 'centre stage' in several of the frames. He is the central character in frame 1, and the first one to crawl through the hole in frame 3, although in the later frames (4 and 6), he is the one on the left. I also wondered what had happened leading up to the drinking session, and why Darren portrayed himself in dark glasses. We did not have the opportunity to discuss these aspects, as he was sent to prison at his next court appearance.

In this example, the actual execution of the comic strip was a major work and must have taken considerable time and thought. It required a commitment that Darren certainly did not have when he first agreed to do it, and the very fact that he had at last been able to 'commit himself on paper' showed he was ready to make a step towards acknowledging his problems and doing something about them.

Seeing Other People's Points of View

In several cases, the comic strips provided an opportunity to look at the situation from an objective outsider's point of view. Tim had a long history of driving offences, and spent three sessions drawing a twenty-frame comic strip. As he drew, he attributed malevolent motives to other drivers: 'The Toyota was trying to force me off the road'. I looked at his picture and replied 'It looks to me as though the Toyota is simply turning left'. This was a totally new idea to him.

Another client, Len, felt very aggrieved at being arrested while watching others commit a burglary. I asked him to draw out the sequence, and then look at the scene as if he were the policeman on the beat. He realised that the policeman would assume all those present (before they ran from the scene) were equally involved.

So far I have given examples of work with individuals. However, this method can be used equally well with groups, in a slightly more structured form. The next section describes two different group situations.

Examples in Practice: Groups

Alcohol Education Group

Many probation services run 'Alcohol Education Groups' for clients whose offences are related in some way to alcohol. Most of these groups are regarded as educational in orientation, giving information (via films and exercises) about the effects of alcohol, and providing an opportunity to discuss these. At the end of the group (a series of eight sessions) clients can choose whether to go for treatment at a centre, to do some individual work with their probation officers, or to do nothing at all.

When it was my turn, with a co-leader, to run one of these groups, we found that we had a large group (14) and this made it difficult to get discussion going. Moreover, several of the group made it clear they were only attending because of the court order and were not willing to participate actively, making it difficult for those who did want to gain something from the group. In order to foster more active participation, we decided to abandon the film allocated for the session on 'Alcohol and Crime' and substitute a drawing session.

Each group member was given a large sheet of paper and oil pastels. They were all asked to divide their paper into four, and then to show themselves drinking in frame 1 and being arrested in frame 4. The intervening frames were to show how they got from the initial situation to the final one.

Figure 8.6 shows Kevin drinking with friends in a pub after a meal elsewhere. They drank a lot, then drove to someone else's house, and finally Kevin drove home, and had an accident with another car. He remembered nothing more about getting home except climbing into bed, and was very surprised when the police came to arrest him the next day. Later he realised he must have done what they said, and admitted it.

Another group member's drawing (*figure 8.7*) showed Fred and a friend drinking in a pub. When they came out, the friend was still upright, but Fred had scribbled out his own legs to show he was 'legless'. He was then persuaded to break into a lorry and steal things, and was caught at it by a police car, ending up in a police cell on his own.

As it was a large group, members were asked to share their work in pairs and seemed to enjoy this as well as the actual drawing. It was a lively meeting for a group which was usually fairly apathetic. Doing the drawings enabled everyone to participate equally, and the concrete results provided material for discussion. This exercise also helped to bring home to them in a personal way the connection between their drinking and the resulting offences, and helped them to start to recognise their own responsibility for what had happened.

Figure 8.6 - Alcohol and crime: 'Who, me?'

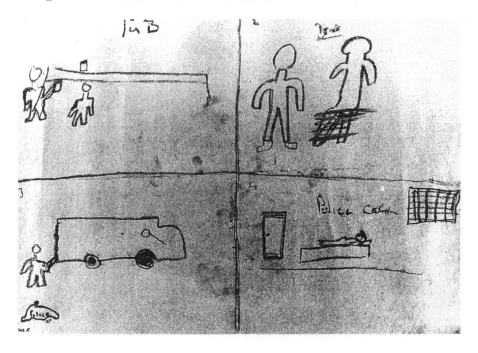

Figure 8.7 - Alcohol and crime: 'Legless'

Probation Women's Group

This group was set up for women probation clients, to enable them to discuss some of the common factors causing them to offend, such as poverty and family problems. It was felt that this would be beneficial in helping these women (who are often isolated at home) feel that they were not alone. Group members played a large part in choosing the topics for discussion, and at one point embarked on a series of sessions on different aspects of crime.

As part of this series, the women were asked to think of a crime committed by themselves or someone else they knew (so that they could protect themselves if they wished) and draw three pictures: the circumstances before the crime, the crime itself, and the consequences.

Figure 8.8 - Shoplifting and loneliness

Section 1 in *figure 8.8* shows Christina in the middle, in great distress, but unable to talk to her family, who seem to be unaware of how she is feeling. Her mother, to whom she had talked a lot, had died four years previously, and she felt she had not replaced this company. Section 2 shows Christina shoplifting, and section 3 shows her, very frightened, in front of the magistrates. There were good consequences, in that her husband and grown up children realised she needed someone to talk to, and her husband accompanied her shopping lest she be tempted to shoplift again. However, she felt this would not arise, as she would make the effort to talk to her family about problems, and felt confident they would respond.

Figure 8.9 - Shoplifting and family problems

Figure 8.9 starts with a depressed family living in a cramped flat, totally unsuitable for three children under five, with money problems at the top of the agenda - they had no money at all. Maria is saying 'Help!'. In section 2, Maria is being escorted by a policeman into a police car, then to prison (behind bars) and finally to court. She felt too ashamed to depict her actual crime of shoplifting, which was committed to overcome the lack of money, and was condoned by her husband. She was caught and fined, but then felt she had to shoplift again to pay off the fine. Section 3 shows a newspaper (top left), because she was frightened her case might be reported. However, the family is a good deal happier, as she has been put on probation and has achieved a transfer to a house with a garden (and a swing!). The family had also been referred to child guidance for help with their marriage and discussion on how to bring up the children, and Maria felt this was supportive too.

As the group was fairly small, the women shared their pictures with the whole group. The general discussion threw up a lot of material, particularly concerning difficulties with their children, the lack of friends with whom to talk things over, money problems, and so on. The process of doing the pictures seemed to bring these things into the open, and enabled everyone to contribute. In this way they also came to feel less ashamed, as they acknowledged factors in common, which were often beyond their control. From this they moved on to how to change their circumstances, or to find ways in which they could exercise greater control over their lives.

These two groups show how the use of a sequence of pictures can help group members look at their own stories and also to discuss common factors that come to light. This can lead on to further art therapy sessions to look at topics which are important to group members.

Developments into Further Work

The initial work using strip cartoons to portray the offence can lead in many different directions. Some unfortunate clients lead such chaotic lives that even this initial work remains unfinished, as further offences or homelessness overtake them. For those who are more stable, there are sometimes obvious directions for further work: reduction of alcohol consumption, social skills practice in making friends, or marital counselling, for instance.

There may also be ways forward using art as a medium for counselling, and this can often be very fruitful. The following examples show how this can be used to explore the more general problems lying behind offending.

Figure 8.10 - Bad memory of father

Figure 8.11 - Walking away from violence

Don: exploring and conquering violence

With Don, I continued to use art as the basis for all the other work. Over the next six months, he did over thirty pictures concerning many situations and people relating to his experiences of violence, both as perpetrator and victim. These included family incidents, his father's violence, happy memories, fears and fantasies, his views of girls and boys, and being bullied.

At one point, following Don's thoughts, I asked Don to do pictures of a good and bad memory of his father. *Figure 8.10* shows the bad memory, with Don's father drinking and beating him up. Blood is pouring out of Don's nose, mouth and chest. We discussed the way his family and school all assumed he would grow up like his father, and looked at the possibility of trying to have the 'good bits' without including the 'bad bits'. Don seemed to think perhaps he could.

Don continued to keep his appointments regularly and we made a chart of his behaviour at work. After three months he achieved an incident-free week and was proud of his complete wage packet. He also told me proudly he had walked away from some bother the previous week, so I asked him to draw it for me (*figure 8.11*). He felt good about doing this, and doing the picture seemed to consolidate his new-found belief that he could change, and also look forward to a different destiny from his father.

Carol: a crisis of confidence

Carol was a smart-looking woman of 43, who had been in trouble with the law for several small offences over the years. Her most recent offence was of theft and assault, which she had denied. She had been accused of shoplifting, and instead of allowing her bag to be inspected, first tried to leave and then lashed out at a store detective who tried to apprehend her. She was found guilty and given a two year probation order. She found it hard to talk about her offences because she felt so ashamed of them, but when she did, she linked them with being influenced by others, and going along with things she knew were not right. She felt she often acted in a guilty unconfident way.

To explore these things further, we used pictures. Carol was also trying to leave a poorly paid job, but although she had found another one, she felt she could not make a decision. *Figure 8.12* shows how she felt - metaphorically stuck in a wheelchair, arms pinned to her sides, screaming. I asked her what kept her there, and she said migraine, and portrayed this, describing it as 'thick blackness with a line and flashing lights'. Next I asked where she would like to be instead of being 'in a wheelchair'. Carol drew a picture of money, house, holidays, and herself in an aeroplane. I wondered what stopped her, and this

Figure 8.12 - 'Stuck'

Figure 8.13 - Family of origin

prompted a picture of her family, all spread out, not talking to each other. Next she drew the family as it should be, everyone communicating with each other, and fulfilling the appropriate roles. Finally I asked her to portray her family of origin (*figure 8.13*), and she drew her mother at the left (seated and deaf), then her father, who did whatever was physically necessary but showed no warmth to his children, and then all the children. Carol was the youngest (by far) of eight brothers and sisters, and her parents seem a long way away. Her mother occupied a similar 'stuck' position to Carol herself in the first picture.

Carol realised as she was doing these drawings that what stopped her from doing more positive things was herself, her dislike of herself, and her feelings of being no good. We decided to explore where these feelings came from.

Directly after this session, Carol took the new job on offer to her. She enjoyed it, started to relax, and the migraines lessened. Over the next few months she did about twenty pictures. When she looked back over them just before her order finished, she could see her life 'displayed'. There were good as well as bad things, and she seemed more able to accept the 'ups and downs' and feel she had some control over her life.

Conclusion

I hope I have shown how one simple method of using strip cartoon drawings has a particular application to looking at crime events, which to participants often seem to 'just happen'. The process can then be inspected by clients who can observe themselves in the drawings from an outsider's point of view. By slowing down the process, and having it displayed in front of them, clients are also more able to decide the points at which change is feasible. This can help them to decide on small practical changes which can give them more control over their lives and make it less likely that they will re-offend. However, this is usually a long process, and the initial comic strips often show up the underlying problems which need to be tackled. Some of these too may be approached using art.

Although I started with the idea of using art in general with probation clients, I found that the 'comic strip' format seemed to have a particular application to discussing crime events. It has proved acceptable to many clients, and has been useful in providing information from the client's point of view - including aspects not usually obvious from verbal accounts. This has helped me to work more realistically with clients, and has also shown up the variety of factors which may lie behind crimes.

As clients draw their pictures, they include themselves as actors at the centre of the story rather than as victims of circumstances. They begin to see themselves as responsible people who have some control over their actions, including their offending, and their future.

Chapter 9

Art Therapy and Homeless People

Clare Swainson

Introduction

This chapter looks at the way art therapy has become an important part of the mental health services being offered to homeless people in Bristol's inner city. It starts with some background information on homelessness and the types of mental health and associated problems presented by clients, and the setting up of the Inner City Mental Health Project. I will look at our experience in establishing art therapy groups as a response to identified needs and at the request of members of the client group. This will include a description of three art therapy groups, in a men's hostel, a women's hostel and at the Project's base. The chapter concludes with a case study involving friendship between two members of an art therapy group, and the way this influenced their pictures.

Homelessness

Although a percentage of homeless people sleep rough and therefore literally have no roof over their head, the term 'homeless' is also used for those people who have no secure, permanent home of their own. They may live in hostels for homeless people, 'Bed and Breakfast' (B & B) accommodation, or substandard accommodation. The homeless population includes transient people, temporarily homeless people, and others who have lived in the same hostel almost continuously for long periods of time. One of my clients has lived in the same hostel for fifteen years apart from brief periods in hospital or B & B accommodation.

Very few people find themselves homeless through choice. There are many reasons why someone may lose their home. These include family break-up brought about by a variety of causes, for example domestic disputes or bereavement; physical and mental illness; long-term residence in an institution, eg a children's home, hospital or prison; alcohol or drug dependency; unemployment and job redundancy. Behind these personal reasons lie changes in government policy, particularly in the field of benefits. For example, young people under eighteen who cannot stay at home are not eligible for financial support.

Being homeless is a crisis situation for anyone. Being a woman and homeless is an especially vulnerable position. The problems that lead women to this desperate situation include violence or abuse from parent or partner; incest; pregnancy; rape. Many will have mental health problems. Some women are bailed to a hostel by the courts.

Research has shown that the longer people remain homeless the more difficult it is for them to find and keep permanent accommodation. Homelessness increases their existing problems and often leads to the development of new ones. Homeless people frequently have complicated histories and may have been involved with a large number of agencies during their downward spiral. Their problems and health difficulties are likely to be long-term.

Though clients often fall into more than one category with regard to their mental health problem, six main categories can be identified:

1) psychoses (acute psychotic episodes, eg schizophrenia, paranoia);

2) behavioural difficulties (inappropriate behaviour or actions misunderstood by others);

3) alcoholism/drug abuse;

4) organic brain disease/damage, eg dementia;

5) learning difficulties in addition to mental illness;

6) mental health problems due to homelessness (Appleton, 1989).

The Effects of Homelessness

Homeless people are viewed in a very negative way by society, as of no value, unhelpable and difficult. There is a very real stigma attached to homelessness which dehumanizes people. With poor prospects of gaining employment and accommodation, feelings of hopelessness set in, followed by feelings of worthlessness which lead to despair, apathy and low motivation. In the long term, homeless people's ability to relate to others becomes severely impaired, and they may have very few or no significant relationships in their lives. They often feel extremely lonely and isolated even if living in a hostel with many others, and suffer from lack of confidence in their social skills, feeling unable to communicate with other people.

Workers in this field can be seriously affected by the hopelessness felt by clients and the difficulties experienced in making any headway. Staff morale is consequently often low, leading to a high turn-over of staff members. This lack of continuity makes it even more difficult for clients to build up the trusting relationships they need.

Facilities available

Despite the very visible nature of their problems, homeless people have a very low profile and get little attention from society in general. Though there is much good will among both statutory and voluntary agencies, there are still few services available to homeless people. The Bristol Cyrenians run the only day centre in the area specifically for homeless people and have some accommodation to offer. They also run an outreach service to people sleeping on the streets. The Cyrenians and the Inner City Mental Health Project (ICMHP) are the chief agencies offering a service to homeless people.

The Inner City Mental Health Project (ICMHP)

The ICMHP was set up in 1987 with money made available to health authorities by the Department of Health and Social Security. This money was to fund work which the local health authority wished to develop but for which it lacked financial resources. A condition of the funding was that the primary client group should be the seriously and long-term mentally ill. The funding was to be for a period of three years, after which the local health authority would include it in their budget.

Within Bristol the geographical area identified as being in particular need was the inner city. Both research findings and clinical experience showed the inner city as having high social stress indicators and high psychiatric morbidity, yet it was proving difficult to provide a mental health service for the area. The ICMHP was to:

a) make an assessment of various needs within the area;

b) attempt to respond to those identified needs;

c) attempt to make existing services more 'user friendly' while also offering a further 'user friendly' service itself;

d) plan innovative provision which would more adequately meet the situations encountered in this area of Bristol. (Phillips, 1988)

Two areas of work were established as the Project's priorities:

1) to improve relationships between statutory health provision and mi-
nority ethnic groups within the inner city;

2) to increase the service offered to homeless people within the area.

The Project is under constant evaluation, having its own evaluation officer in
addition to being evaluated by the DHSS. The Project is also in constant
consultation with a wide variety of bodies via a large steering group and a
smaller consultative group. Discussion has also taken place through public
meetings in the community which the Project serves.

The Inner City Mental Health Team (ICMHT) consists of twelve workers
covering the Afro-Caribbean, Asian and homeless sectors. I work in the
homeless sector which also has a homeless development worker, a life skills
worker and some input from two support workers. In two of my groups I am
assisted by volunteers from Community Service Volunteers. We also have a
senior art therapist for one session a week.

My involvement

I attended the first public meeting in November 1987 and talked to both clients
and ICMHT members concerning the possibility of art being used in the
Project's work. The response was favourable but nothing definite was pro-
posed. In the January of 1988 I set up an art therapy group in a women's hostel
at the request of staff there. Shortly after this, Peter, the homeless development
worker of the ICMHP, approached me with the offer of the Project's support
and the possibility of another group in a men's hostel. Over two years my
involvement has grown and I now work 21 hours on a temporary contract, in
both art therapy and life skills groups.

Why Art Therapy Groups?

Before the setting up of the ICMHP, Peter, the homeless development worker
(HDW), had been working with homeless people in his capacity as a community psychiatric nurse. Through this contact he had become aware that some
of his clients had previously enjoyed art-based activities (in a variety of settings
including hospitals and day centres). When the Project was getting off the
ground, he canvassed those homeless people under his care and the response
confirmed his feeling that art therapy groups would prove useful to many from
this client group. That art therapy has such a high profile in the work of the
ICMHP is very much a reflection of the importance placed on listening to

clients. It was our hope that art therapy groups would facilitate social interaction, motivating individuals by giving the opportunity for self-exploration and expression, to people whose verbal skills are sometimes limited.

The lives of these people are poverty-stricken in more than the material sense. The art therapy group can enrich their lives on several levels. On the personal level they have the opportunity to express feelings safely. This is particularly useful where anger is concerned, as the inappropriate expression of anger is a major problem in the hostels. Consequences for the client can be serious. Clients often have very high anxiety levels and can find the group an aid to relaxation. The group can also help them to get in touch with their creativity and capacity for spontaneity. A great deal of confidence-building and self-validation can take place, with the possibility of increased insight and self-awareness. The art therapy group also works on a social level. Through their involvement in the group, members can grow in awareness and recognition of each other. This can lead to an appreciation of one another and in consequence more communication and cooperation. The group is a place where they can feel support and trust, not only from the group worker but from each other.

Setting up

We decided to begin by engaging people within the hostel setting. The service was therefore being offered literally 'on the spot', requiring minimal effort on the part of clients interested in attending. It also meant clients were visibly reminded each week of the existence of the group, an important part of getting the group accepted into their weekly structure. Homeless people tend to lead very aimless lives. Eventually, when the group has been running consistently at the same time and place for long enough, it becomes a part of the hostel structure.

Also to be overcome is clients' distrust and their very natural wariness of people coming in from 'outside' to offer a service. With long-term residents, time is on our side and I have found it possible to build good trusting relationships with them. With the more transient clients it is more problematical and I often feel unsure of what progress there has been before they move on.

In order to set up groups within the hostels, it was vital to gain the interest and support of staff working there. When staff appreciate and value the aims of the group it helps enormously, both on a practical level and that of emotional support for client and group worker. Many hostel staff had little or no experience of this type of group. I found the most effective way of engaging them was to get them painting alongside clients. At the women's hostel this has proved particularly successful, leading to the request that we run an art therapy day workshop for their staff team. This method of engaging workers has also worked well with members of the ICMHT. Those team members who have had the opportunity to paint within a group both gain personally and are more likely to see the benefits their clients could experience if referred to such a group.

Most of our referrals come from the voluntary sector including the hostels and the Cyrenian Day Centre. Referrals also come from statutory bodies such as the health centre, social services, hospitals, and other sectors of the ICMHP. In addition we have seen an increasing number of self-referrals, which is indicative of the trust in the service being offered that now exists amongst the homeless.

A year after setting up the first group, we were running four hostel-based groups, while art also formed part of the content of several other groups held in community centres and at the Project's base.

Also held at the base was an art therapy group where it was possible for clients to do more intensive work than was possible within the hostel setting.

Group in Hostel for Homeless Men

The hostel has beds for 130 men under the care of four care assistants. We receive more referrals from this hostel than from any other agency. Referrals consist almost entirely of residents with long-term mental health problems.

Setting up

A weekly clinic was being held at the hostel by Peter, as the homeless development worker. It was therefore decided that the group should run in the same time slot as the clinic so that Peter could introduce new referrals from his clinic while also being on hand if I should need support. The first members of the art therapy group were all residents who had been seeing Peter on a one-to-one basis at this clinic for some time.

Negotiations with the hostel started in February 1988. The group met for the first time in April 1988. In the initial stages Peter spent short periods of time with the group but once it was well established his place was taken by a support worker. The support worker was eventually replaced by a volunteer.

The group

The group is a 'referral-only' group, for long-term residents with serious long-term mental health problems, and is consistently full to capacity. Eight group members is the ideal number, as the aim is a small group in which I and my assistant can give good attention to all group members during the course of a session. All the group members attend on a voluntary basis. The group is ongoing - some members have been attending since its inception. Alongside those members who have been a part of the group for some time, there are usually one or two who only attend for a short time due to a variety of reasons including: eviction from the hostel; deterioration of mental and physical health; and hospitalisation. The group takes place in the afternoon and runs for three hours. This includes the setting up and clearing away periods.

The hostel gave us the use of a disused dormitory in which to set up the group. We have had to move rooms several times, which has caused problems. Group members become confused and it can lead to feeling marginalised by the hostel. For much of the time the room in use by the group has also been used as a store room, and on occasion we have had to share our space with vast quantities of clothing, mattresses and margarine. Despite these problems we manage to create a friendly safe place with the facilities offered by the hostel.

Both I and my assistant may spend some time painting. Joint painting is particularly useful for engaging some clients - worker and client working together on the same painting. One of the advantages of workers painting is that we can model, for the clients, ways of using materials and ways of looking at issues through images.

The session

Some group members will be waiting when I arrive, others will gradually drift in during the setting up period. They are encouraged to help in putting out the paint and choosing music. We start with a cup of tea or coffee and it is at this point that common themes can emerge from their conversation. This may suggest a starting point for their painting. The amount of time individuals spend painting varies considerably. Some group members will spend only a short time painting and then sit and chat or watch others at work. Other group members will paint until the last minute. I spend some time with each member giving them the opportunity to talk about their painting or anything else they may wish to share.

Benefits

Encouraging group members to take responsibility for the group through helping with the clearing up, making tea and coffee etc, is an important part of the group process. Hostel life removes the opportunity for residents to do even the simplest domestic chores, while also removing many areas in which choices can be made and personal autonomy exercised. Of course painting itself is also an area in which they have the freedom to make decisions, to experiment and try out ideas.

For many, this group has been the first step towards engaging with other people. Despite living surrounded by others, residents rarely talk to one another and can be very isolated. This is particularly true of those long-term residents with chronic mental health problems. Group members have shown an interest and concern for one another which has led to increased contact between them outside the group setting. The majority of group members had not been attending groups anywhere else prior to coming to the art therapy group. Since attending this group, many have gone on to attend other groups run by the ICMHP or at the Cyrenian Day Centre.

Group in Hostel for Homeless Women

This hostel is considerably smaller than the men's hostel, having beds for only eleven women plus second stage accommodation consisting of six bedsits. It is one of the very few places in Bristol offering emergency accommodation to homeless women. Women are referred to the hostel by various voluntary and statutory agencies. There are also a large number of self-referrals. Very few women stay long as the hostel aims to move women on into more permanent accommodation. Women's ages range from 16 to 30 years. The staff team of four workers and project leader offer a key worker system plus twenty-four-hour cover.

The group

The art therapy group was set up in January 1988. It differs from the men's group in that it is open to all the hostel's residents, and to ex-residents and women living in the bedsits. The numbers attending can therefore fluctuate from week to week. When women leave the hostel but remain local, they have the option to continue attending the group to help in the transition from hostel life to living on their own. The group operates in the hostel's kitchen and this puts a limit on the number that can attend at any one time. Four women is a comfortable number, making six with myself and the volunteer who assists me. However, throughout the three hours that the group runs, women come and go, so that up to eight women can actually make use of the session. As with the group in the men's hostel, the art therapy group in the women's hostel has to wrestle with many practical difficulties. A session of the women's group is very similar in structure to the men's group.

Benefits

Elements such as age, gender and size of hostel combine to make this group feel very different from the men's group. However, the women's gains in many cases correspond with those of the men. Good work has been done on the appropriate expression of feelings and the building up of women's self-esteem.

The atmosphere at the women's hostel can seem very volatile at times and the art therapy group acts as an oasis in its midst. Even when police and ambulance crew have invaded the building, the group has run, providing an important point of normality. Suicide attempts are sadly a fairly frequent occurrence, and the group provides a space for women to express and explore their feelings around such an attempt by themselves or a fellow resident. This can lead them to an understanding of how their actions can affect others. When an ex-resident, well known to some of the residents, killed herself, the group provided a very important space for them to express their grief, to talk about their friend, to remember her in their painting, and to express their anger both at her and at those they thought had failed her.

Obviously the venue and the fact that group membership is not always constant affects how women use the group. This has not negated the value of the group; there have been occasions when women have done very intense work. The group also provides pointers for areas women could usefully work on in their key working sessions.

The Wednesday Group

Setting up

Once art therapy groups were well established in several hostels it was felt that a group in a different setting would enable clients to work at a more intense level than was possible in the hostels. An art therapy group was therefore set up in a community centre, initially with three workers; a senior art therapist, Peter (HDW), and myself. A great deal of work had to be done by Peter in order to get the group off the ground: visiting prospective group members and encouraging them to attend; following up if they ceased attending; advertising the group amongst other agencies and so on. Much of this work continues to be necessary and, without it, the group would not exist. Peter no longer attends the group but meets regularly with the senior art therapist and myself to exchange information and review methods of working.

The group is open to referrals from the Afro-Caribbean and Asian sectors as well as the homeless sector of the ICMHP. Initially most referrals came from the homeless sector but that changed gradually and the group is now representative of all the Project's client groups. A new venue was partly responsible for this change. The community centre was not very satisfactory, and after some months we moved the group to the Project's base. Thus the group became more visible to ICMHT members. It has therefore received more attention, which has had a positive effect on referrals and the way art therapy is perceived by the team.

The Wednesday Group took a long time to get established and this tried our patience sorely. The group ran for two months with no clients. In retrospect this early period without clients was very valuable as it gave us, the workers, the opportunity to try out ways of working together. When clients started attending the group, we had developed a comfortable format, and were also feeling at ease with one another as a working team. The group structure also proved to be congenial for clients and therefore, with some small changes, has remained much the same.

The group

The group is limited to six members plus two workers. It runs for two and a half hours and starts with a chat over tea or coffee. As described in the men's hostel group, this period often throws up issues which then influence the content of group members' paintings. Occasionally the senior art therapist uses a theme or organises a group painting. Group members and workers paint for about an hour, after which there is a group sharing period. Our participation was particularly important in the early days, when there was only one client, as it prevented the client from being isolated as the one being 'done to'. It also helps prevent worker/client, well/ill polarisation. Now that the group is running at full strength, I and the other therapist continue to paint, but are less likely to talk about our paintings.

As with the hostel groups, we encourage group members to take a degree of responsibility for the group, helping with clearing up, deciding ground rules, for example, about smoking in the group. They are also asked, once they have decided to come, to make a commitment to attend the group regularly.

A Friendship

The case I have chosen to describe is not in any sense 'typical', I do not feel there can be 'typical cases' when we are working with very different individuals whose only common denominator is their lack of a home. However, it is a case which reflects our aspirations for the art therapy groups, and describes a friendship between two men who attended the art group in the men's hostel.

Clive has been resident at the hostel for about two years, after spending more than thirty years in a hospital for people with learning difficulties. He is 65 and has no family members still living. Though Clive left hospital voluntarily, he looks back on that period in his life as a happier time than the present for him. He was able to work at the hospital and there were many organised social activities. Since living in the hostel, he had become very withdrawn and interacted little with other residents or staff.

Simon is much younger than Clive, being in his early twenties. He had suffered some brain damage through solvent abuse and was on medication for problems associated with this. He was also still sniffing glue. Simon had family but was not in touch with them, not knowing where they were.

Clive was introduced by hostel staff to the art therapy group in its second week and has attended constantly since that date. Simon also started attending the group in its early days, after being referred by Peter.

From the beginning Clive produced recurring themes in his paintings. There were objects he knew how to draw and from which he got a sense of his own skills. There was the OXO box in 3D which his grandfather had taught him to draw, fruit of all kinds and space rockets. Often they would all turn up in the same painting, drawn in a simple manner with heavy outlines which he then filled in with paint. In the early days these would be interspersed with images remembered from his past. It was these past memories which caused much of his current distress, and this became apparent when I talked to him about his painting.

Clive was always one of the first to arrive for the group and one of the last to leave. He had a sense of responsibility towards the group, washing out his own paint palette and brushes, and encouraging others to do the same. To him it was important that group members kept to the ground rules while in the group, such as 'no scrounging for fags or money', clearing up afterwards etc. He also went to collect one of the older group members who liked to be woken up from his after-lunch nap in order to attend the group. Clive took on this role of 'responsible core member' gradually, and his relationship with Simon was part of this process.

Simon's behaviour in the group was the antithesis of Clive's. He appeared to take no real interest in the rest of the group, only approaching another group member if he wanted to break the 'no scrounging' rule. He drank vast quantities of coffee so that we ran out of milk. The combined appeal of group members and myself to leave enough for everyone else made little impact on him. Simon

Figure 9.1 - Clive's painting

Figure 9.2 - Simon's drawing

always created a lot of mess at his table but would never clear it up. He tended, therefore, to become a focus for other members' anger.

I found it difficult to make any real contact with Simon. Approaches by me tended to be met with a smile but little else. His conversation was monosyllabic and I gauged his feelings from his behaviour rather than from any words. There was sometimes evidence that he had been glue-sniffing from glue on hands and arms, a kind of 'absence' in his eyes, and the way his drawing was affected. Simon's concentration was not good and his drawing always rather desultory, and on bad days there would be very little of it. Simon rarely drew recognisable objects but covered part of a sheet of paper with many short straight pencil lines. He sometimes covered these with paint, usually black.

When both men had been attending the group for several weeks, I noticed that Clive always chose to sit at the same table as Simon, and it was clear that a relationship was gradually developing between them. Two months later, I observed Clive's concern for Simon. Clive was expressing anger at Simon's continued glue-sniffing, very aware of the dangers involved. He made it clear that he knew a great deal about Simon's movements - from whom he borrowed money, where he bought the glue and where he went to sniff it. It was therefore evident that Clive's feeling of involvement with Simon extended outside the group. Five months from the start of this relationship, Clive and Simon were obviously spending time together outside the group setting.

Clive also took an interest in Simon's drawing though he didn't consider it very good. He would encourage Simon to look at his own (Clive's) drawing and attempt something similar. On Simon's better days he would occasionally follow Clive's lead. The two paintings illustrated show an example with Simon (*figure 9.2*) attempting to draw motifs from Clive's painting (*figure 9.1*), in this case rockets and OXO boxes.

Indeed, Clive appeared to be the only group member who could make any impact on Simon, both in regard to his picture-making and his behaviour. Though Clive would spend part of every session scolding Simon, there was also a playful element to their relationship. They would sometimes play pat-a-cake type games with their hands, always a cause for much laughter.

Whilst Simon's behaviour in the group seemed dictated by how much he was glue-sniffing, Clive's appeared related to how Simon was. The relationship with Simon seemed to help Clive become much more animated, indeed positively chatty. His paintings had also grown in variety and colour during this period. However, on days when Simon was particularly agitated, Clive withdrew and his picture-making suffered.

During late summer, though the friendship was being maintained, Simon's behaviour and health were deteriorating. I took a week's holiday in September and arrived back to find there had been some animosity between Clive and Simon during that week. However, they sat together as usual in the group, and when anger was expressed, it was over Clive's usual bugbears, the mess Simon made and the paucity of his drawing.

However, by the end of September, Simon just stared blankly when I spoke to him, and gave no response. He expressed animosity towards others and was constantly agitated, filling small areas of his paper with short abrupt pencil marks. In what was to prove his last session, at the beginning of October, he drew very little and shouted at Clive for the first time in the group. Clive then also became agitated, talking to himself at the window rather than sitting at the table with Simon. He took a long time to put pencil to paper and I had to help him make a start. For the first time he left his painting, of two trees in Autumn, unfinished.

On arriving at the hostel the following week I found that Simon had been evicted. He had never missed a session of the art therapy group, and the gap seemed huge. I felt particularly concerned for Clive, who had lost a friend. Clive arrived an hour late, and was quiet and somewhat forlorn. He finished his autumnal picture, painting leaves falling to the ground and grey clouds scudding across the sky. It was a cold and desolate painting.

From the beginning I had felt that Clive was the prime mover in this relationship, and the friendship had certainly had a very positive effect on him. For Clive there was value in the comparison that he could make between himself and Simon. Observing Simon's drawing gave Clive the opportunity to appreciate his own picture-making skills, and feel good about his own achievement. There were also opportunities within the relationship for Clive to feel an increase in self-esteem. The group was also influential in improving Clive's quality of life, giving him a place where he was appreciated, his contribution valued, not mocked. He was listened to, encouraged and praised, not only by myself and my assistant but also by other group members. As a result Clive visibly blossomed. However Simon was his particular friend, and Clive really felt his absence keenly.

I am not sure how far Simon was able to appreciate this friendship. There was certainly a connection between Clive and Simon that I could not achieve between myself and Simon. He attended every week, so both the group and his friendship with Clive had been of some value to Simon during his stay at the hostel.

The eviction of a client can feel like a failure on my part. At times like these, I have to look again at what our realistic aspirations for group members are. Even a short-term improvement in quality of life is better than none. For some like Clive, that improvement may allow quite a change to take place, and this may prove to be long term.

Conclusion

Working in this field we have to accept that radical change for individuals is unlikely. In many cases they have learnt to adapt to the life they live, and are poorly motivated to attempt change when they see little chance of success. Their pessimism is founded on reality in that resources are scarce, and very few will be able to move into their own home or more appropriate accommodation than they currently occupy. In many cases we are therefore limited to enabling clients to cope better with their current environment rather than enabling them to move into more suitable accommodation. In this context the art therapy groups have been a success, benefiting clients on a personal and social level. Without a dramatic increase in resources available to homeless people we, the workers, must learn to be pleased with what from the outside might appear to be small successes. Even the smallest improvement in quality of life is a cause for celebration. The art therapy groups have certainly provided that.

Bibliography

References

Appleton, P. (1989) *ICMHP Report from the Development Worker in the Homelessness Sector*. Bristol: Inner City Mental Health Project.

Appleton, P. (1989) *ICMHP Report from the Worker in the Homeless Sector*. Bristol: Inner City Mental Health Project.

Berne, E. (1964) *Games People Play*. Harmondsworth: Penguin.

Crick, L. (1988) 'Facing Grief'. *Nursing Times* No. 27.

Dalley, T. (ed) (1984) *Art as Therapy*. London: Tavistock Publications.

Donnelly, M.J. (1984) 'You're Good at Dealing with Difficult People'. *Inscape* (Journal of BAAT) 2(13)

Donnelly, M.J. (1988) 'Psychotherapy and Psychosis in an Out-patient Setting'. Unpublished.

Fromm, E. (1951) *The Forgotten Language*. New York: Holt, Rhinehart & Winston.

Greenwood, H. and Layton, G. (1987) 'An Out-patient Art Therapy Group'. *Inscape* (Journal of BAAT) 1(12).

Heaton-Ward, W.A. (1977) *Left Behind*. Plymouth: Macdonald & Evans.

Kings Fund (1987) *Facing the Challenge*. London: Kings Fund.

Liebmann, M. F., (1986) *Art Therapy for Groups*. London: Croom Helm.

Macleod, R. (1988) *Footsteps and Heartbeats Album*. (LP record)

Mian, I.H. (1985) *Psychiatry of Old Age Service*. Bristol: Southmead Health Authority.

Miller, A. (1987) *The Drama of Being a Child*. London: Virago (originally published in 1979).

Moreno, J.L. (1969) *Psychodrama (Vol. III). Action, Therapy and Principles of Practice*. New York: Beacon House.

Perls, F. (1969) *In and Out the Garbage Pail*. New York: Bantam Books.

Perls, Hefferline and Goodman (1951) *Gestalt Therapy*. New York: Julian Press.

Phillips, J. (1988) *ICMHP Interim Report of Project Officer*. Bristol: Inner City Mental Health Project.

Pitt, B. (1982) *Psychogeriatrics - an Introduction to the Psychiatry of Old Age*. London: Churchill, Livingstone.

Rowe, D. (1983) *Depression: The Way Out of Your Prison*. London: Routledge and Kegan Paul.

Southmead Health District (1987) 'Introductory Guide to Goal Planning with People Receiving Long-term Mental Health Care'. Unpublished paper: Gloucester House, Southmead Health District, Bristol.

Storr, A. (1979) *The Art of Psychotherapy*. London: Secker & Warburg/William Heinemann.

Thomson, M. (1989) *On Art and Therapy*. London: Virago.

Warren, A. (1988) 'A Brief Introduction to the Community Rehabilitation Service for Southmead'. Unpublished paper.

Further Reading

A: Art therapy and related areas

Adamson, E. (1984) *Art as Healing*. Coventure, London, and distributed in the US by Samuel Weisen Inc., York Beach, Maine.

Bach, S. (1969) Spontaneous Paintings of Severely Ill Patients. *Documenta Geigy, Acta psychomatica*, Basel: J.R. Geigy, S.A.

Barnes, M. and Berke, J. (1971) *Mary Barnes: Two Accounts of a Journey Through Madness*. London: MacGibbon and Kee.

Betensky, M. (1973) *Self-Discovery Through Self-Expression*. Springfield, Illinois: C.C. Thomas.

British Association of Art Therapists (1989) *Art Therapy Bibliography*, 11a Richmond Road, Brighton.

Cardinal, R. (1972) *Outsider Art*. London: Studio Vista.

Carrell, C. and Laing, J. (1982) *The Special Unit, Barlinnie Prison: Its Evolution through its Art*. Glasgow: Third Eye Centre.

Case, C. and Dalley, T. (eds) (1990) *Working with Children in Art Therapy*. London: Tavistock/Routledge.

Dalley, T. (ed) (1984) *Art as Therapy: An Introduction to the Use of Art as a Therapeutic Technique*. London: Tavistock/New York: Methuen.

Dalley, T. and Gilroy, A. (eds) (1989) *Pictures at an Exhibition: Selected Essays on Art and Art Therapy*. London: Tavistock/Routledge.

Dalley, T. et al (1987) *Images of Art Therapy*. London: Tavistock.

Di Leo, J. (1983) *Interpreting Children's Drawings*. New York: Brunner/Mazel.

Dubowski, J. (ed) (1984) *Art Therapy as a Psychotherapy in Relation to the Mentally Handicapped?*, 1984 conference papers, Hertfordshire College of Art and Design, St. Albans.

Edwards, B. (1982 & 1979) *Drawing on the Right Side of the Brain*. London: Fontana/Collins, 1982, Los Angeles: J.P. Tarcher Inc., 1979.

Edwards, B. (1986) *Drawing on the Artist Within*. London: Fontana/Collins.

Edwards, D. (1987) 'Evaluation in art therapy', in Milne, D. (ed) *Evaluating Mental Health Practice*. London: Croom Helm.

Ehrenzweig, A. (1970) *The Hidden Order of Art*. Englewood Cliffs, New Jersey: Prentice-Hall.

Franck, F. (1974) *The Zen of Seeing*. London: Wildwood House, Massachusetts: Harvard University Press.

Franck, F. (1980) *The Awakened Eye*. London: Wildwood House.

Fuller, P. (1980) *Art and Psychoanalysis*. London: Writers and Readers.

Furth, G.M. (1988) *The Secret World of Drawings: Healing through Art*. Boston: Sigo Press.

Gardner, H. (1980) *Artful Scribbles: The Significance of Children's Drawings*. New York: Basic Books.

Goldsmiths College Students, *As We See It: Approaches to Art as Therapy* (available from British Association of Art Therapists, 11a Richmond Road, Brighton).

Goodnow, J. (1977) *Children's Drawing*. London: Fontana, Open Books.

Harris, J. and Joseph, C. (1973) *Murals of the Mind*. New York: International Universities Press.

Hill, A. (1945) *Art Versus Illness*. London: Allen & Unwin.

Hill, A. (1951) *Painting Out Illness*. London: Williams and Northgate.

Jameson, K. (1968) *Pre-School and Infant Art*. London: Studio Vista.

Jung, C.G. (1964 & 1968) *Man and His Symbols*. London: Aldus/Jupiter, and New York: Dell Publishing Co. Inc.

Kellog, R. (1970) *Analysing Children's Art*. Palo Alto, California: National Press.

Keyes, M.F. (1974) *The Inward Journey*. Millbrae, California: Celestial Arts.

Klepsch, M. and Logie, L. (1982) *Children Draw and Tell*. New York: Brunner/Mazel.

Kramer, E. (1978) *Art as Therapy with Children*. New York: Schocken.

Kramer, E. (1981) *Childhood and Art Therapy*. New York: Schocken.

Kwiatkowska, H. (1978) *Family Art Therapy*. Springfield, Illinois: C.C. Thomas.

Landgarten, H.B. (1981) *Clinical Art Therapy*. New York: Brunner/Mazel.

Landgarten, H.B. (1987) *Family Art Psychotherapy*. New York: Brunner/Mazel.

Leuner, H. (1984) *Guided Affective Imagery*. New York: Thieme-Stratton.

Levick, M. (1983) *They Could Not Talk and So They Drew: Children's Styles of Coping and Thinking*. Springfield, Illinois: C.C. Thomas.

Liebmann, M.F. (1986) *Art Therapy for Groups*. London: Croom Helm (now published by Routledge).

Linesch, D.G. (1988) *Adolescent Art Therapy*. New York: Brunner/Mazel.

Luthe, W. (1976) *Creativity Mobilisation Technique*. New York: Grune and Stratton.

Lyddiatt, E.M. (1971) *Spontaneous Painting and Modelling*. London: Constable.

Milner, M. (1971 & 1967) *On Not Being Able to Paint*. London: Heinemann, 1971, New York: International University Press, 1967).

Naumburg, M. (1966) *Dynamically Oriented Art Therapy*. New York: Grune and Stratton.

Naumburg, M. (1973) *An Introduction to Art Therapy*. New York: Teachers College Press.

Nicholson, S. (1976) *Interactive Art and Play*. Milton Keynes: Open University Press.

Oaklander, V. (1978) *Windows to Our Children*. Moab, Utah: Real People Press.

Pavey, D. (1979) *Art-Based Games*. London: Methuen.

Prinzhorn, H. (1972) *Artistry of the Mentally Ill*. New York: Springer-Verlag, (translated from Bildnerei der Geisteskranken, Springer, Berlin, 1922).

Quinn, T. (ed) (1989) *Art Therapy for People with Severe to Marginal Learning Difficulties*. 1989 conference papers, Leicester, obtainable from BAAT.

Rhyne, J. (1984) *The Gestalt Art Experience*. Chicago: Magnolia Street Publishers.

Robbins, A. and Sibley, L.B. (1976) *Creative Art Therapy*. New York: Brunner/Mazel.

Rubin, J.A. (1978) *Child Art Therapy*. New York: Van Nostrand Reinhold.

Rubin, J.A. (1984) *The Art of Art Therapy*. New York: Brunner/Mazel.

Rubin, J.A. (ed) (1987) *Approaches to Art Therapy*. New York: Brunner/Mazel.

Samuels, M.D. and Samuels, N. (1975) *Seeing with the Mind's Eye: The History, Techniques and Uses of Visualisation*. New York: Random House.

Selfe, L. (1977 & 1978) *Nadia: A Case of Extraordinary Drawing Ability in an Autistic Child*. London: Academic Press, 1977, San Diego, California: Academic Press Inc., 1978.

Stevens, J.O. (1973) *Awareness*. New York: Bantam Books.

Thomson, M. (1989) *On Art and Therapy*. London: Virago.

Tilley, P. (1975) *Art in the Education of Subnormal Children*. London: Pitman.

Ulman, E. and Dachinger, P. (eds) (1976) *Art Therapy in Theory and Practice*. New York: Schocken.

Ulman E. and Levy, C.A. (eds) (1980) *Art Therapy Viewpoints*. New York: Schocken.

Wadeson, H. (1980) *Art Psychotherapy*. New York and Chichester: John Wiley.

Wadeson, H. (1987) *Dynamics of Art Psychotherapy*. New York and Chichester: John Wiley.

Wadeson, H., Durkin, J. and Perach, D. (eds) (1989) *Advances in Art Therapy*. New York and Chichester: John Wiley.

Weiss, J.C. (1984) *Expressive Therapy with Elders and the Disabled*. New York: The Haworth Press.

Williams, G.W. and Wood, M.M. (1977) *Developmental Art Therapy*. Baltimore: University Park Press.

Wohl, A. and Kaufman, B. (1985) *Silent Screams and Hidden Cries: An Interpretation of Artwork by Children from Violent Homes*. New York: Brunner/Mazel.

B: Other expressive arts, creativity and psychotherapy

Combined arts therapies

Anderson, W. (ed) (1977) *Therapy and the Arts: Tools of Consciousness*. New York: Harper & Row.

Feder, E. and Feder, B. (1981) *The Expressive Arts Therapies: Art, Music and Dance as Psychotherapy*. Englewood Cliffs, New Jersey: Prentice-Hall.

Jennings, S. (ed) (1983) *Creative Therapy. 2nd edition*, Banbury: Kemble Press.

Jennings, S. and Minde, A. (1990) *Art Therapy and Dramatherapy: Their Relation and Practice*. London: Jessica Kingsley Publishers.

Warren, B. (1984) *Using the Creative Arts in Therapy*. London: Croom Helm, Cambridge, Massachussetts: Brookline Books.

Creativity

Gordon, R. (1978) *Dying and Creating*. London: Society of Analytical Psychology.

Lowenfeld, V. and Brittain, L.W. (1970) *Creative and Mental Growth*. London: Collier-Macmillan.

May, R. (1976) *The Courage to Create*. London: Collins, New York: Bantam Books.

Storr, A. (1977 & 1985) *The Dynamics of Creation*. Harmondsworth: Pelican, 1977, New York: Atheneum, 1985.

Dance movement therapy

Lamb, W. and Watson, E. (1979) *Body Code: The Meaning in Movement*. London: Routledge and Kegan Paul.

Levete, G. (1982) *No Handicap to Dance*. London: Souvenir Press.

Payne West, H. (1983) *An Introduction to Dance Movement Therapy*. ADMT Publications, 99 South Hill Park, London NW3 2SP.

Dramatherapy

Grainger, R. (1990) *Drama and Healing: The Roots of Dramatherapy*. London: Jessica Kingsley Publishers.

Jennings, S. (ed) (1987) *Dramatherapy: Theory and Practice for Teachers and Clinicians*. London: Routledge.

Jennings, S. (1990) *Dramatherapy with Families, Groups and Individuals: Waiting in the Wings*. London: Jessica Kingsley Publishers.

Langley, D.M. and G.E. (1983) *Dramatherapy and Psychiatry*. London: Croom Helm.

Music therapy

Alvin, J. (1978) *Music Therapy*. London: Hutchinson (and distributed in the US by State Mutual Book and Periodical Service, New York, 1984).

Nordoff, P. and Robbins, C. (1977) *Creative Music Therapy*. New York: Harper and Row.

Priestley, M. (1975 & 1984) *Music Therapy in Action*. London: Constable, 1975, St. Louis, Missouri: MMB Music Inc., 1984.

Play therapy

Axline, V. (1973 & 1976) *Dibs in Search of Self*. Harmondsworth: Penguin, 1973, New York: Ballantine Books, 1976.

Axline, V. (1989) *Play Therapy*. Edinburgh: Churchill Livingstone.

Kalff, D. (1985) *Sandplay*. Boston, Massachusetts: Sigo Press.

Lowenfeld, M. (1979) *World Technique*. London: Allen & Unwin.

Winnicott, D.W. (1980 & 1982) *Playing and Reality*. Harmondsworth: Penguin, 1980, New York: Methuen, 1982. Originally published 1974.

Psychotherapy

Dryden, W. (ed) (1989) *Individual Therapy in Britain*. Milton Keynes: Open University Press.

Dryden, W. (ed) (1989) *Handbook of Counselling in Britain*. London: Routledge and Kegan Paul.

Freud, S. (1962) *Two Short Accounts of Psychoanalysis*. Harmondsworth: Penguin.

Jung, C.G. (1963) *Memories, Dreams, Reflections*. London: Routledge and Kegan Paul.

Milner, M. (1988) *Hands of the Living God: Account of a Psychoanalytic Treatment*. London: Virago (first published 1969).

Rowan, J. and Dryden, W. (ed) (1988) *Innovative Therapy in Britain*. Milton Keynes: Open University Press.

Winnicott, D.W. (1978) *The Piggle: Account of the Psychoanalytic Treatment of a Little Girl*. Hogarth Press.

Stories and Writing in Therapy

Bryant, J. (1985) *Anybody Can Write: A Playful Approach to Writing*. US: Whatever Publishers.

Casterton, J. (1986) *Creative Writing: A Practical Guide*. London: Macmillan Educational.

Gersie, A. and King, N. (1990) *Storymaking in Education and Therapy*. London: Jessica Kingsley Publishers.

C: Art therapy journals and organisations

Journals

Inscape, the Journal of the British Association of Art Therapists, obtainable from BAAT, 11A Richmond Road, Brighton, BN2 3RL.

The American Journal of Art Therapy (published in association with the American Art Therapy Association), Vermont College of Norwich University, Montpelier, Vermont 05602, USA.

The Arts in Psychotherapy, an international journal, Pergamon Press, Maxwell House, Fairview Park, Elmsford, NY 10523, USA.

List of Contributors

Karen Drucker trained for her Masters Degree at Pratt Institute, Brooklyn, New York. She works as Senior Art Therapist, on a part-time basis, in a community out-patient unit in Southmead Health Authority, including working in a psychogeriatric day hospital and a psychogeriatric in-patient ward.

Tish Feilden works as a freelance psychotherapist and trainer. She works with individual adults, couples, families and children. She also runs art therapy groups. After studying psychology, sociology and education at degree level she undertook research in art therapy and went on to train as a psychotherapist.

John Ford is Head Art Therapist at Glenside Hospital where he has worked for the last ten years, working with a broad range of people from out-patients to long-stay patients. He maintains an interest in other approaches to therapy beside art, more specifically Gestalt and Psychodrama.

Edward Kuczaj qualified as a Registered Nurse in the field of Mental Handicap, then left to pursue an interest in Fine Art. He worked then as an Art Instructor at Hortham Hospital before being seconded to the part-time Art Therapy course at St Albans. He works currently at Hortham Hospital as a Senior Art Therapist.

Marian Liebmann is a qualified teacher, social worker and art therapist. She has had a varied career, and has used art therapy in a day centre, community groups and in her current work in probation. She is the author of *Art Therapy for Groups*, which arose from her research for an MA in Art Therapy.

Sarah Lewis trained as a sculptor and has used art as a way of working with people in different settings: a playgroup, schools, with ex-offenders and community workers. She qualified as an art therapist in 1986 and is employed as a community-based art therapist in adult psychiatry for the Northern Sector of Southmead Health District in Bristol.

Claire Skailes originally trained as an art teacher and worked as Art Therapist at Coney Hill Psychiatric Hospital, Gloucester, where she is now Head of Department. She has an MA in Art Therapy and has contributed papers to conferences in London and Budapest.

Clare Swainson originally trained as a Norland Nanny before taking a change in direction and gaining a Degree in Fine Art at Bath Academy of Art. As a trainee art therapist on the part-time Diploma in Art Therapy at Hertfordshire College of Art and Design, St Albans, and worker with Bristol's Inner City Mental Health Project, she has developed art therapy with homeless people.

Roy Thornton has worked for many years in a wide variety of adult psychiatric settings. He is a Specialist Adviser to the Council for National Academic Awards for the validation and monitoring of those art therapy courses not in universities. He has also worked on the Association's core course requirements with the BAAT Education Committee. He teaches, lectures and gives workshops to a wide variety of institutions and professional bodies.

Index

Art Therapy with Offenders

Edited by Marian Liebmann

Foreword by Stephen Tumim

ISBN 1 85302 171 7

'If the Prison Service is to fulfil its stated duty "to help prisoners lead law-abiding and useful lives in custody and after release," this book must be one of the more important guides on how to achieve it. ...art therapy with offenders seems both necessary and desirable at this stage of regime development, and each chapter in this book provides fresh ideas for it.'

— Judge Stephen Tumim

'Each chapter stands in its own right, and authors set out very clearly what they intend to say. Each work setting is vividly described, giving the reader a sense of what it must feel like to work in such settings... There is a wealth of information on the 'nuts and bolts' of establishing oneself in an institution, inviting referrals, setting up a group sessions, making contact with clients, introducing them to the medium and documenting the process of therapy... I felt these accounts to be as useful to music therapists as art therapists, and relevant to therapists setting up work with any client group, not just offenders...I found so much to stimulate and inspire me, and little to criticise... This book demonstrates the value of art therapy with offenders.'

— Journal of British Music Therapy

'The foreword by Judge Stephen Tumim sets the scene for a thoroughly good book... It is in essence a practical and pragmatic series of essays offering new horizons about art as a vehicle for the understanding and addressing of offending behaviour... Each contributor whilst adding their own dimension appears to reflect a common thread. A book of reference as well as ideas...those involved in the training of prison and probation staff would do well to find a place for this book on their reading list. What it is not, is a book for the Art Teacher alone. It has much more to offer.'

— AMBOV Quarterly

'*Self and Society* readers will find this superb book a valuable contribution to in-depth work in their therapy and with themselves...brilliant and beautiful collection of papers and illustrations.'

— Self and Society

'...a valuable insight into how the setting for therapeutic work shapes its from and potential... There are interesting contributions from art therapists working with adolescent sex offenders.'

— Assoc for Child Psychology and Psychiatry Review and Newsletter

'An extensive reading list adds to the value of this comprehensive book as a resource for work with offenders.'

— A Journal of Reviews and Commentary in Mental Health